CW01512672

Love
Marriage
Divorce

Garry Johnson

NEW HAVEN PUBLISHING LTD

Published 2018
NEW HAVEN PUBLISHING LTD
www.newhavenpublishingltd.com
newhavenpublishing@gmail.com

Editor Ed Collis

Cover design © Pete Cunliffe
pcunliffe@blueyonder.co.uk

DEDICATIONS

I would like to thank

John Baron MP
John Hemming MP
Lord Justice Munby
Sue Reid
Judge Moloney
Diane Pryor
Justine Salmon
Sarah Reynolds
Jerry Lonsdale
Alan Foskett
Judge Roderick Newton
The Freedom of Information Act
Sam, Adam, Lucy

Taking on the establishment isn`t easy but I did it to change things

Content

A Message to My Daughter — 9

The Facebook Dad — 32

The Freedom Fighter — 38

The Cockney Rebel — 54

Love Marriage Divorce — 80

I Fought the Law — 114

False Allegations — 128

Working Class Hero — 134

Life after Adultery — 144

The Fight Goes On — 151

Serial Killer — 159

We Are Family — 170

Questions for My Daughter — 184

Life after Death — 197

So Who Is Your Dad — 202

Me and Mr Brown — 204

Fatal Attraction — 207

Witness of Abuse — 211

Introduction

This is the true story about me, Garry Johnson, the only man in Great Britain to take on and defeat Social Services.

They tried to silence me. They tried to intimidate me. They tried to destroy me.

They tried to kill me.

I was arrested 5 times, twice sent to prison and spent 29 days in a coma and on a life support machine.

Every time they knocked me down, I got straight back up.

I went to The High Court where Lord Justice Munby ruled in my favour.

When the barrister for Essex Social Services stood up to object he was told: "Whatever you say I will not change my mind".

Adding:

"There are no longer any restrictions on Mr Johnson".

Judge Moloney ordered Essex Social Services to hand over all their documents.

Judge Roderick Newton ruled I could legally tell my story.

This is it.

"The truth the whole truth and nothing but the truth so help me God."

Garry Johnson

A Message to My Daughter

I am nothing like Thomas Markle or the feckless fathers who appear on The Jeremy Kyle Show and give men a bad name.

"So why does my daughter not want to see me?" is the question I ask myself every day.

I have not seen her since July 2008 and this October 3rd will be Lucy's 18th Birthday.

She becomes an adult and deserves the right to know who I am.

After 10 years of forced separation I think I also deserve the opportunity to introduce myself.

Not by re-writing history and producing a `whitewash`.

Altering facts and hiring highly paid lawyers in pin-stripe suits to manipulate the truth.

This is a factual account and not some biased or flawed Government report written by Alistair Campbell.

I will introduce myself by telling the truth, the whole truth and nothing but the truth.

This is a story I've been waiting to tell since December 2013.

Case Number: CM14P00300

On December 13th, 2013 at Chelmsford County Court in Essex Judge Roderick Newton followed in the illustrious footsteps of Lord Justice Munby (The High Court) and Judge Moloney (Southend) by ruling in my favour.

He removed the `Gagging Orders` on every aspect of my private and personal life.

I could now legally tell my side of the story but because of the adult content decided to wait.

I did not want to expose my 13-year-old daughter to stories about sex, drugs and rock & roll.

She was too young.

I wanted to protect her from reading about the violence, harrasment and intimidation.

I decided it was best to wait until my daughter came of age and entered the adult world.

The 16th of December 2013 at Chelmsford County Court was an historic day in British legal history.

Judge Roderick Newton ruled that Garry Johnson could legally write his autobiography with no subject `out of bounds`.

I could talk about anything and everything My life, my ex-wife, my children, my 8-year war with Social Services

This included putting the record straight about pornographic films like `Saturday Night Specials`, East End gangster novel `Till Death Us Do Part` and lies about my mental health.

At last I could reveal how my reputation had been ripped to shreds for 8 years with no right of reply.

I was smeared more times than Jeremy Corbyn and the victim of revenge porn.

As well as being a great victory for the `freedom of the press`.

It also gave hope to other victims.

The thousands of decent, innocent parents (mums & dads) from all over the UK who`d also been used and abused by the corrupt family courts.

It was a win for every victim of harassment and intimidation committed by goose-stepping stormtroopers from Social Services.

Sadly I couldn`t attend court in person as I was otherwise engaged.

I was in a coma and on a life support machine in Basildon Hospital.

I was there in spirit and such was the power and strength of my argument I won the case.

Judge Roderick Newton must have been impressed by the crafting of my statement.

It was I must admit a `work of art`.

A classic use of the English language which flowed like a Sir Winston Churchill speech.

So theatrical it could have been written by Oscar Wilde.

On the day the written word really was mightier than the sword.

It spoke louder than a vocal recital performed by a Welsh male voice choir.

I suggested in my statement:

"Writing my autobiography without mentioning every detail about my marriage & divorce would be like Sir Geoff Hurst penning his and not mentioning the World Cup winning Hat-trick".

Adding:

"How could Sir Paul McCartney write his memoirs and ignore The Beatles or David Bowie without paying tribute to Ziggy Stardust?"

A lovely turn of phrase I thought and the Judge agreed.

I wish I`d been there to witness this judicial climbdown.

To treasure the moment, soak up the atmosphere and hear the verdict in person.

But to quote a famous old saying goes, `you can`t be in two places at the same time`.

As Judge Roderick Newton was making his historic ruling an army of angels and heroic NHS staff were battling to keep me alive.

One of the first things I remember hearing after waking from my month-long coma was my eldest son Sam saying:

"Dad we won, we won. I opened your letter from the court and we won.

Dad you did it".

As well as bringing bunches of grapes and bottles of drink Sam continued to bring good news.

The next day:

"Dad, I`ve got a message from Sue, she told me to tell you we`ve won".

Such was the state of my medical condition it was quite a few days before I understood what he meant.

It was only when Sam read aloud the content of the Court Judgement that the penny dropped.

The magnitude of the decision finally sunk in.

I was free to lift the lid on Essex Social Services. I could expose the corrupt Family Courts.

I could legally write a hard-hitting and thought provoking `kiss and tell`.

It had been a long-time coming but now had the final piece of the jigsaw.

A smoking gun with more fire-power than a KGB hit squad.

Legal permission from the British Courts to inform the world of my plight.

Lord Justice Munby, Judge Moloney and Judge Roderick Newton had given me the power to tell the true story of my life and times.

I was on a winning roll.

I'd twice survived `dying` and more victories were just around the corner.

I was transferred from Basildon to Billericay Hospital for a month of rehab.

My speech had returned but not my ability to walk.

After 24 hours in a private room with a TV and my own shower Sam and Adam arrived with more luxuries.

They also brought a letter from home.

It was from Helen Lincoln the Head of Essex Social Services which read:

"Dear Mr Johnson,

Regarding the allegations about Mr Grimson. It is clear that child protection procedures were not followed with sufficient rigour.

This shortcoming needs to be recognised."

It had taken the courts and Essex Social Services 8 years to admit they'd made a mistake.

The courts had over-stepped the mark and been `out of order` to censor the truth.

Essex Social Services wrong to ignore the facts.

They had deliberately turned a blind eye and a deaf ear to the truth.

Ignoring the fact that my three children had been violently threatened and verbally sexually abused by the boyfriend of my ex-wife.

Essex Social Services underestimated me as I'm living proof that you shouldn't judge a book by its cover.

I talk like a character on EastEnders but I'm not thick. I was smart enough to enlist the help of two MPs.

I was sharp enough to win.

I've waited 5 years to tell my story because of the adult content.

In December 2013 my daughter was a 13-year-old teenager.

I'm going public now because October 3rd 2018, will be her 18th birthday.

I want her to know the truth and everything there is to know about her dad.

Every detail about his past, private, personal and professional life.

It`s risky as she might not like what she reads but it`s a risk I`m willing to take.

What have I got to lose?

She already hates the `made-up` version of me.

The pantomime villain that never existed.

The `mad, bad and dangerous` monster invented by Social Services.

If my daughter is going to hate me I`d rather it be the real me, not the fictional character created by her mum. The single dad who brought up her brothers and spent 13 years fighting to see her.

The dad twice sent to prison who almost died fighting to see her.

The dad who would do it all over again.

The dad who never stopped loving her.

The man who wants her to know nothing would make him happier then to be her dad again.

The dad whose dream is to have his children all together in the same room.

The dad with a lump in his throat, fighting back the tears as he wrote the last few sentences.

Lucy must be told the truth, the whole truth and nothing but the truth.

There`s no other way for her to independently decide if she wants me back in her life

If she wants us to be father and daughter again.

All I want is one chance to prove I am honest, loyal and trustworthy.

I would never lie to her. I`m many things but I`m not and have never been a liar.

I want Lucy to know everything I say is the truth, the whole truth and nothing but the truth.

I can show her the documents which explain exactly why she`s been kept from me.

If after reading this book she still has any doubts I`d willingly take a Lie Detector test.

I`d even go on national television and put my reputation on the line.

How?

I`ve already contacted The Jeremy Kyle Show and asked about taking a Lie Detector Test.

I`ve spoken on the phone and exchanged a number of emails with a lady called Mia.

She knows my story.

I have nothing to hide.

Can my ex-wife say the same?

I ask the same question of her boyfriend and social worker Peter Brown?

Are they scared of the truth?

Would the three of them be prepared to take a Lie Detector test and answer questions on live TV?

I`d jump at the chance.

There is nothing I would not do for the chance to be reunited with my daughter.

I would put my life on the line.

I`ve proved in my 8-year war with Essex Social Services that I`ll fight to the death.

There was nothing I would not do to keep custody of my sons.

I want Lucy to know that I`m here and have always been here for her.

Although a devout atheist I still pray to God that one day we`ll be reunited.

I had spent 8 years attending courts all over Essex fighting for contact and only stopped because of serious illness.

The fact is `dead men can`t talk`.

They can`t defend themselves against smears or protect their reputation.

The family of war hero Lord Brammell will confirm that.

As will the loved one`s of all those dead celebrities smeared in politically motivated hatchet jobs.

I will only have `peace of mind` and die `happy` if I know everything about me is on-the-record.

I am `so to speak` putting it all down on paper before it`s too late.

Can you even imagine the lies and smears my ex-wife and her family would spread if I was dead?

They would crucify me and I`d have no right of reply.

I`ve not seen my daughter for ten years and in case we never meet I need an insurance policy.

I want her to know I was one of the `good guys`.

A romantic rebel, a doting dad, an eccentric day dreamer who was never `mad, bad or dangerous`.

At no time in my life was I ever mentally ill and have 4 expert medical opinions to prove it.

I am/was to quote my friends and family:

"A funny fella, a genuine working-class rebel, slightly eccentric, great company and well worth getting to know".

My daughter has grown-up on a diet of lies and old-fashioned propaganda.

A childhood of inhaling fake news.

Thirteen years of brainwashing.

Every child has the right to know his or her Father.

My daughter has been denied that basic human right.

It was morally a criminal act.

Essex social services were partly responsible for this crime.

They took part in the `brainwashing` and the poisoning of her mind.

Social Worker Peter Brown willingly conspired with my ex-wife to cover-up the truth.

Since 2005 my daughter has been programmed and conditioned to hate me.

Her mother refusing any form of contact including phone calls, Birthday cards, letters and emails.

I have hundreds of legal documents proving that statement to be true.

So why was I and why am I being denied the right to be her dad?

You don`t have to be a member of Mensa or a `Brain of Britain` champion to know the answer of that question

It wasn`t just a pincer movement of my ex-wife and Social Services attacking me.

They fired the guns but the smiling faces loading the bullets were the Taylor Family.

My in-laws did not have a good word to say about me in 15 years of hostilities.

They were anti-me throughout our marriage so weren`t going to start saying nice things after we`d divorced.

Even a Trump supporter could work that out.

They never accepted me and I was never good enough for their precious daughter.

My in-laws were by nature bitter and twisted people. They were life-long bigots. They hated my independent nature and what they considered my `annoying habit` of always questioning their old-fashioned beliefs.

In any discussion on whatever topic I always took the opposing view.

My view of the world was not theirs and certainly wasn't appreciated.

Mr Taylor would always mock me because I was half-Irish but didn't drink.

He`d say:

"It`s just my luck, my daughter gets herself married to the only Irish man who doesn`t drink".

He thought it was unmanly.

The annoying thing was I was `more of a man` than he`d ever been.

A former `Jack the Lad` who`d done things he couldn't even dream of doing.

Had he indulged in group sex, cocaine parties and all sorts of illegal activities?

Mr Taylor was so straight he wouldn`t watch Television if he didn't have a TV licence.

I didn't need to drink pints of bitter in The British Legion or get drunk in a Working Men`s Club to prove to him I was `one of the boys` and a `real man`.

I`m not boasting, well maybe a little but I`d had more women in a year then he`d had in a life-time.

Taken more illegal drugs then he`d taken aspirins and frequented the best clubs in London.

Had he ever been to Stringfellows, Annabelle`s or The Playboy Club?

I`d enthusiastically lived the sex & drugs & rock & roll lifestyle for 10 years yet he had the cheek to mock me because I was virtually teetotal.

It was my choice to be stone cold sober and drug free.

I wanted to be a `great husband` and the `best dad in the world`. Not his drinking buddy.

I stopped drinking 3 or 4 weeks after Sam was born.

I didn't need stimulants to make me happy anymore.

I was high on life.

I can still remember where and when I quit taking substances and alcohol.

It was Manchester 1992.

I`d been sent up North to review a Bryan Adams open air concert at Maine Road.

Manchester City`s old football stadium.

His act was the same but I wasn't the same person who saw him at the Hammersmith Odeon in 1985.

That night I went to the after-show party and was buzzing out of my box.

1985 was a great year. I was 9 stone with dyed blonde hair and cheekbones to die for.

I took vast quantities of cocaine and went home with Joan Jett lookalike Erica Echenberg. I loved being on the road and partying it was the best thing about the job.

Who wouldn`t enjoy hanging out with rock stars, models and groupies?

But that night in Manchester everything changed.

The last thing I wanted was another night of sex, drugs and booze.

I didn`t want to be there. I was missing Julie and Sam and wanted to go home.

I went to bed early and got up early so I could catch the first train back to London.

That was the night I quit as a music journo and re-invented myself as a TV pundit.

There`d be no more long distance travelling and nights away from Julie and Sam.

I enjoyed being sober and my new life as a dad.

I wasn`t going to the pub and drinking pints of beer just to please my former father-in-law.

I couldn't give a Monkeys whether he thought I was a `real man` or not.

Joyce and Tony Taylor really were the in-laws from hell.

Both were born to moan, criticise and interfere in other people's lives.

They gate-crashed my marriage for 15 years and have spent the past 13 brainwashing my daughter.

When Julie and I separated they celebrated first and then seized control of my daughter.

They stole her childhood and taunted my parents.

It was all out war.

They bragged to my Father: "after all we've told Social Services your son will never see Lucy again".

This was followed-up by a phone call to my mum in which my former mother-in-law sneered:

"Garry will never see his daughter again."

My ex-wife then picked-up the phone and taunted my mum saying:

"You won't be seeing Lucy unless my Mother and Father are in the room".

The three of them colluded to keep a dad from his daughter and deny my mum the right to see her granddaughter.

I hope Lucy is smart enough to understand what 'crimes' have been committed in her name.

They conspired with social worker Peter Brown to stop me from seeing my daughter.

They spread more fake news than President Putin's false Facebook accounts.

It didn't matter who they hurt in the process or how many lies they had to tell.

They were as honest as the £350m NHS slogan on Boris Johnson's battle bus.

All that mattered to them was keeping Lucy to themselves. At first they got away with hoodwinking the police, Social Services and the secretive Family Courts.

But what is that famous old saying. The pun that is never wrong?

"The truth will always out".

And eventually it did.

I quote directly from one of the Essex Social Services documents I obtained by using the Freedom of Information Act.

These are the words of Social Worker Rachel Sismey.

She states:

"Sam turned up at the Willowbrook Contact Centre to see his sister.

He brought along a present for his sister and said:

`Hello Lucy, I love you Lucy Johnson` but ignored his mother.

Sam was hugging his sister and then Mrs Johnson pulled Lucy away.

She then started shouting, screaming and swearing at Sam saying:

`Enjoy this moment because it`s the last time you`ll ever see her`

Adding;

`Believe me there is no way you`ll ever see Lucy again`.

Sam froze and was very distressed by the behaviour of Mrs Johnson"."

I last saw Lucy at the same venue before my ex-wife decided not to bring her anymore.

I would sit and wait with Sam and Adam every week but Lucy never arrived.

This went on for months and I have the Essex Social Services documents that prove I`m telling the truth.

I often ask myself. `Is my daughter aware of any of this or was she too young to remember?`

Is she aware her mother got court injunctions to prevent me from visiting or even writing to her?

I was stopped from attending School Sports Days, Concerts, Parents Evenings.

I wasn`t allowed to see copies of Lucy`s Term reports or school photos.

Her mum even got a legal letter preventing Sam, Adam and myself from visiting her in hospital.

Lucy was having a throat operation but the three of us were kept away.

The injunction was delivered moments before we left for the hospital.

I was straight on the phone to my solicitors.

They tried to obtain permission for Sam and Adam to visit without me but the Taylor family refused.

If my daughter or anyone else has doubts they are more than welcome to read the official documents.

This book is a 100 per cent factual account.

It details everything that happened after Garry met Julie in the summer of 1989.

The truth about our 15-year marriage and 13-year conflict since separating.

A bitter feud that can only end when I`ve been re-united with my daughter.

I`ve always believed divorces should be civilised and not involve outsiders.

The Judge agreed saying:

"It is not helpful when a third party is involved, even more so when that person has spoken to the children in such an offhand and disgusting manner".

Spot on.

It`s not fair to ask children to take sides and even more upsetting to introduce them to strangers.

My ex-wife did not see it that way.

Julie could not wait to involve solicitors and Essex Social Services.

She was determined to use the children as weapons.

It was her biggest mistake as any short-term advantage gained back-fired.

It blew up in her face.

Her selfish shoot-from-the-hip behaviour riled me and alienated our sons.

It caused scars that have still not healed, that maybe will never heal.

I was baffled by her behaviour. It was so out-of-character.

Julie had known me for 15 years. She knew me close-up and personal.

I always wore my heart on my sleeve.

Julie knew better than anyone what a `doting dad` I`d always been.

So how on earth could she make such an error of judgement?

Who was it that convinced her I`d just sit back and take it lying down?

Julie was aware of my low-opinion of social workers.

She knew all about my background of being in care and losing my own dad.

The fact I never got over him walking out on me.

Julie must have known I would never give up my children without one hell of a battle.

I'd fight to the death.

She was very badly advised by both her solicitors and her boyfriend.

And God only knows whose bright idea it was to involve social services?

Once they were involved I stopped speaking to Julie and we'll never speak again.

There's been no conversations between her and our sons since 2005.

Involving Social Services was like a red rag to a bull.

Since childhood they had been my least favourite people in the world.

Some people hate the police, blacks, Jews, Muslims, Catholics, homosexuals.

I hated social workers.

It was a life-long hatred and passionately held belief.

I didn't invent it as part of my custody battle.

Julie knew I hated Social Workers. And the reason why.

She was aware of what happened to me when I was thirteen and living in a Children's Home.

I was the victim of an historical sex crime committed by a social worker.

A grown-man, an adult who was meant to be in charge of my welfare.

It happened one Sunday evening and the memory never faded.

I was a victim during my first time at Boyles Court Children's Home at Great Warley, near Brentwood.

My abuser was a social worker who looked like TV comedian Ronnie Corbett.

But he was anything but funny.

I can still remember as if it happened yesterday.

The bastard coming into my room, sitting on my bed and putting his hand under the duvet and touching my private parts.

I can still see his face and remember the rotten smell of the Brylcream in his hair.

I returned to Boyles Court a year later, more like a man than a little boy.

This time I was a big mouthy skinhead and immediately sought him out.

He was still wearing the same checked jacket and sporting a bad Elvis Presley style quiff.

I walked towards him and gave him my very best 'if looks could kill' stare and, let's just say, he didn't come back for a second grope.

I confided in Julie shortly after she moved in. She was the first person I'd ever told.

I had no choice but to bare my soul.

She spotted something was 'wrong' and I didn't want to lose her.

I'd stopped taking drugs so couldn't self-medicate and hide how I was thinking.

Julie wanted to know why at about 8pm every Sunday to quote her "I went weird?".

It was because for about Fifteen minutes I reverted back to the 13-year-old boy at Boyles Court.

I also had something else on mind that happened at around the same time on a Sunday evening.

Aged 12 I witnessed a gang of older boys stripping a 15-year-old girl naked.

I was taking a short cut home through the local park and came across a gang of older boys from my school.

There were half a dozen and recognised some as big brothers of my mates.

As I got closer I could see what was going on, they were keeping watch while 4 others attacked a helpless girl.

She was pinned to the ground and they had removed her clothes.

I didn't know her name but knew her face. This was the first time I'd seen a naked girl in the flesh.

I should have gone to her aid or even called the police, but I wasn't yet a teenager.

At that age you don't know difference between 'grassing' and doing the 'right thing'.

Today as an adult, if I came across the same thing I'd automatically step in and help.

I never blush, but a few year later saw the same girl at a party and couldn't stop blushing.

I was embarrassed in case she recognised me as the skinny little kid who saw her naked.

Since that incident and what happened to me at Boyles Court I`ve always had a pathological hatred for all types of perverts and bullies.

That`s why I was so angry when my ex-wife and Social Services did nothing to protect my children.

Abuse is something I can't forgive or forget.

That`s why I wrote my novel Serial Killer.

The plot is about a woman who gets revenge on a gang of teenage boys who raped her.

I also used my personal experience of Boyles Court and meeting Peter Brown as the inspiration for a song.

One of the tracks on my album `Punk Rock Stories and Tabloid Tales` is called `Newton Brown`.

The chorus is:

"The nonce the ponce the pervert newton Brown/There`s one in every town and always hanging around".

I always draw on my past when I write songs, poems, novels or books.

That same album I recorded with Swedish rocker Sulo Soren Karlsson also has songs about my daughter and ex-wife.

"Father`s Day" for Lucy and "The One That Got Away" for Julie.

I have never been scared of showing or sharing my emotions and always worn my heart on my sleeve. I saw defeating Peter Brown and Essex Social Services as my revenge for what happened to me at Boyles Court.

I`m pretty confident without the involvement of a third party our divorce could have been amicable.

Julie and I could have been the Gwyneth Paltrow and Chris Martin of Essex.

Before the involvement of Social Services my position had always been laidback and liberal.

As it was to life in general.

If there had to be a `fight` I would always want a `fair fight` rather than a David and Goliath situation.

Bullying has no place in my life.

There has to be mutual respect on both sides.

I wanted ground rules that meant no outsiders would ever be involved in our private business.

As in the past we would sort things out between us.

It had worked `pretty well` for 15 years and that`s how I wanted our relationship to continue.

Julie had other ideas.

She wanted a dirty fight and the dirtier the better and started behaving like a bully in the playground.

She had a personality transplant and surrounded herself with a gang.

This included a boyfriend resembling Shrek.

A team of solicitors led by a woman who walked, talked and looked like Angela Merkal.

Social worker Peter Brown who looked like Principal Skinner from The Simpsons and dressed like Mr Bean.

The `gang` included.

Social Services.

The police.

The Essex Criminal Mental Health Team.

Psychiatrists.

The Family Courts.

Cafcass.

Her parents.

A child-abusing boyfriend who carried out a `campaign of terror` against our children.

Julie knew the only thing I hated more than Social Workers was perverts who hurt children.

She`d personally witnessed me shouting at the TV whenever child-killing scum like Ian Huntley or Roy Whiting featured on the news.

Any form of child abuse always affected me badly.

It had always made me angry but once I became a parent it scared me.

I`m not ashamed to admit I even sought medical help for my fear.

I was terrified that something or someone would hurt my children.

I was the most over-protective dad in the world.

In 2000 my anxiety started to get out of control when schoolgirl Sarah Payne was kidnapped and murdered by Roy Whiting.

The double murder in 2002 of Holly & Jessica the 8-year-old girls killed by Ian Huntley freaked me out.

I became a nervous wreck and sick with worry.

Doctor Sims, my GP put me on medication and advised I see a counsellor.

These terrible crimes happened hundreds of miles away so why was I suffering from extreme anxiety?

Sam and Adam were now of an age where they wanted to visit the park on their own.

I was mortified and feared there'd be another Ray Whiting or Ian Huntley hiding in the bushes.

My only mission in life was protecting Sam and Adam.

Years later for being a loving dad I'd be accused of being 'mentally ill'.

What the authorities failed to understand was that I had a very special link with both boys.

Sam was an emergency cesarean and almost died. The first week of his life was spent in extensive care.

I stayed with him night and day.

Julie was also very ill and didn't see him for 5 days so it was me who saw him first.

I was terrified when the nurse told me to put my hands inside the incubator and change his nappy.

My hands were shaking and I was drenched from head to toe in pools of sweat.

I was so wet it was as if I'd just got out of the shower

When we split-up my ex-wife used this against me.

Instead of telling her solicitors and Peter Brown I'd been treated for stress she told them it was for a mental illness.

I went from over-protective dad to being 'mad, bad and dangerous'.

They say 'mud sticks' and it stuck to me for years. I had to fight and fight again' to clear my name.

I was examined and given a clean bill of health by the Essex Mental Health Criminal Team

A psychiatrist in Bellmarsh Prison.

Dr Best from Harley Street.

Dr Black from Laindon Mental hospital saw me three times in 3 years and each occasion gave me 'clean bill of health' saying:

"Mr Johnson is not mentally ill".

So why so many examinations?

My ex-wife would repeat the same allegations to who-ever she spoke to next.

A new Hearing in a different court meant another chance for her to smear my reputation.

This harassment continued for five years.

It was only the 9-page report of Forensic Psychiatrist Dr Sian Llewellyn-Jones that finally got Peter Brown and Social Services out of my life.

She stated:

"Mr Johnson is not mentally ill".

My ex-wife surrounded herself with the sort of people I`ve hated all my life.

Did she honestly believe I`d meekly surrender and runaway like David Cameron the morning after the Referendum?

I eventually got a solicitor who told me:

"From now on Mr Johnson if you`re lucky you`ll get to see your children for a couple of hours every Saturday."

Adding;

"You can take them to McDonalds or Burger King."

Those words of wisdom cost me £350.

I immediately changed solicitors and this time I was advised to lie.

Not directly but was told:

"Mrs Johnson is saying some terrible things about you, so you have to do the same.

If you don't you are in grave danger of losing your children".

I refused.

In my mind if there had to be a fight I still wanted it to be a fair fight.

The children had to come first.

I was very naïve.

I had no idea that divorce lawyers were the lowest of the low and corrupt.

They had no interest in the facts, the truth or the welfare of children.

It`s no surprise that so many members of the legal profession end up as politicians.

The corruption was an eye-opener for me as I'd previously had no involvement with divorce.

I was only Thirteen when my parents divorced.

In 2006 I was told by a barrister:

"The Judge is not interested in the truth.

Family Courts always come down on the side of the Mother".

I replied:

"They won't this time because I have the evidence. It will prove I'm telling the truth".

The reply I got was breath-taking.

I was told:

"Family Courts are not like proper courts of law.

There is no jury and all Hearings are held in secret".

Adding:

"Members of the general public and the press are never allowed access."

He added:

"I know you're a journalist but if you discuss any aspects of your case in public you will go to prison.

You will be in contempt of court".

That is why it has taken so long to get my ordeal into the public domain.

I needed permission of the British Justice system and kept fighting until I got it.

Three separate Hearings and 3 different Judges gave me the green light.

Lord Justice Munby at The High Court in London ruled in my favour saying:

"All restrictions are revoked so Mr Johnson is no longer barred from talking about his sons"

The barrister representing Essex Social Services objected and was told to sit down.

Lord Justice Munby said:

"Whatever your objections I will not change my decision".

At a Hearing in Southend, Judge Moloney ordered Essex Social Services to handover all their files and over-ruled any objections.

Judge Roderick Newton sitting at Chelmsford in December 2013 revoked the `Gagging Order` and granted permission for me to tell my story.

It was a very different world back in 2005.

Tony Blair was still Prime Minister and Donald Trump had his own hair.

It was me against the world. I was a lone wolf suffering in enforced silence.

I wanted a civillised divorce without an ugly custody battle but my ex-wife and former in-laws had decided on all-out war.

The involvement of the boyfriend, Social Services and solicitors changed everything.

I had no choice but to fight the authorities, challenge court orders and ignore injunctions.

Like a wounded animal I came out fighting.

I dug deep and called on all my survival skills to defeat a corrupt system.

I fought with every fibre of my being but the years of resistance came at a price.

It destroyed my health.

I hope my daughter understands why I couldn't continue to fight forever.

My brain was willing but my body wasn't.

I didn't just have the broken-heart you see in films or read about in romantic novels.

I had a damaged heart that is kept working by a plastic valve.

It was according to my consultant the early days of my death sentence.

He could only guarantee me 5 more years.

I had my second triple heart by-pass operation in December 2013 so you work out the mathematics.

That`s why I had to write this book.

I`m still fighting and a dedicated `seeker of truth and justice` but I`ve changed my tactics.

As Sir Winston Churchill our greatest ever war leader said:

"Jaw jaw is better than war war".

There were only so many times I could be arrested or go to prison.

After my triple heart bypass surgery in December 2013 I promised Sam & Adam "no more court cases".

But me being me I had to have `one last hurrah`.

It`s not in my mature to give up.

In April 2014 and against the boys wishes, they were worried about my health, I decided to try again.

I contacted Chelmsford Court.

It was about the 20th time in 8 years that I`d applied for contact with my daughter.

I was visited by Cafcass who are like the para-military wing of Social Services.

If social workers are Nazis than Cafcass staff are more like Gestapo officers.

These people are more secretive than the Freemasons.

The visit did not go well.

Sam and Adam had called it correctly. Healthwise I was not ready for another court battle.

I didn't have the physical energy or mental strength to fight on without doing myself serious harm.

Cafcass were delighted.

They sent me a copy of their advisory report for the court.

It recommended `no contact` stating "Mr Johnson is in poor health and too vulnerable to see his daughter".

I told you these people were pure evil.

These would stop a child visiting a dying parent on his or her death bed.

If social workers are heartless the people employed by Cafcass are ruthless.

More bad news would follow.

A letter from a Southend based solicitor on behalf of my ex-wife saying:

"Lucy wants to get on with her life and doesn`t want to see you".

I have no idea if my daughter said that or even if she knew I`d been trying to see her since 2008

I still don't know if she ever received my Birthday or Christmas cards.

So much I need to know. So many reasons to write this book.

I`m not proud that I stopped fighting Cafcass and attending court but had no option.

What use would a `dead dad` be to Sam and Adam?

It had nothing to do with fear of the courts or not wanting to see my daughter.

I had responsibilities to Sam and Adam.

It wasn't fair on them having the police banging on the door at all hours.

They were in my care and every time my ex-wife had me arrested or locked-up I had to find a safe house for them to hide.

I was incarcerated 6 times and twice sent to prison

The stress of not seeing my daughter and fighting for contact destroyed my health.

I had 5 heart attacks, 2 triple heart by-pass operations and a stroke.

I have the hospital letters and scars to prove it".

This book has three functions.

To expose the corrupt family Court system and introduce a dad to his daughter.

It's also a book every parent involved in a bitter divorce or a battle with Social Services should read.

I'd like to think of it as a self-help manual.

It proves if you fight hard enough and don't let the bastards grind you down you can't be beaten.

Like all bullies in every walk of life they don't like it when you fight back.

I say to all parents.

"Whatever the severity of the odds stacked against you never give up".

All you need is a total belief in your cause and right on your side.

Children are special and it's our duty to protect them at all times.

Know your enemy.

Social Services are pathological liars, the Family Courts secretive and Cafcass corrupt.

They form an evil trinity whose only function is to destroy lives and ruin families.

Like a bank robber with a mask or KKK bigot with a hood they have something to hide.

Why is every case held behind closed doors and never witnessed by the media?

The middle-class people who boast British justice is the best in the world have never been on the receiving end.

That's because there the posh bastards dishing it out.

Family courts are a battlefield built by chinless wonders to promote class war.

The judges, solicitors and social workers are 99% Conservative with an in-bred hatred of the working-class.

Their ancestors were slave owners, landed gentry and robber Barons.

They are among the most powerful forces in the land but I've proved they are not unbeatable.

A lot has changed since my ex-wife and her army of bullies declared war on me.

Lord Justice Munby is now Head of the UK Family Division and the system is far more open than it was back in 2005.

A week is a long time in politics and 13 years is a lifetime in the history of Family Courts.

They are still biased and corrupt but less like a KGB show trial.

Social workers still behave as if stormtroopers at a Nuremberg rally.

Cafcass foot soldiers are the ISIS volunteers of tomorrow.

Imagine a world where Family Courts embraced democracy and open justice.

Social workers having to explain themselves and give evidence in front of a Judge, Jury and Press Gallery full of truth-seeking journalists.

How would the likes of Peter Brown perform in front of campaigning journalists like Sue Reid, Dame Camilla Cavendish and Jane Moore.

All three do what journalists do best. They ask questions and expose any wrong-doing.

Sue of The Daily Mail, Camilla of The Times and Jane of The Sun all helped during my darkest days.

As did The Sun's legendary Agony Aunt Deirde Saunders.

My Roll of Honour includes John Baron MP, John Hemming MP and the boys Solicitor Alan Foskett.

My Legal Adviser Ian Ashby.

Family Law expert and Children's Advocate Jerry Lonsdale who spent many unpaid hours working on my case.

The Facebook Dad

Secret Court Jails Father For Sending Son Greeting On Facebook was the newspaper headline.

A Father had been jailed at a secret court hearing for sending a Facebook message to his grown-up son on his 21st birthday.

How do I Know?

I was that Father.

A political prisoner in 21st century Great Britain.

From secret arrests to secret court hearings, the principle of openness that has underpinned British justice for centuries is being eroded at an alarming rate.

But there is something particularly terrifying about a father whose only `crime` was to inadvertently break a draconian court order, by posting a message about his son`s birthday on Facebook, being sent to prison in secret.

Removing a person`s liberty is the gravest sanction the State can impose. To do so for such a pathetic reason chills the blood.

What was the message that led to a man with a serious heart condition being handcuffed and shackled to a hospital bed?

Why were 2 prison officers guarding the entrance to his room?

2013:

Campaigning journalist Sue Reid wrote:

"Garry Johnson, breached a draconian gagging order which stops him publicly naming his son, Sam, whom he brought up and still lives with him.

In a case which is certain to fuel concerns about Britain`s shadowy network of secret courts, a judge sent the punk poet to prison for contempt at a closed-doors family court hearing in Essex.

He was not arrested by the police or even represented by a lawyer.

The order silencing Garry Johnson, which follows an acrimonious divorce eight years ago, means he cannot mention either of his boys, 21-year-old Sam and Adam, 18, in public, even by congratulating them in a local newspaper announcement when they get engaged, married or have children in the future.

The extraordinary gag is set to last until the end of his life, although his boys are now adults.

Last night they condemned their Father`s jailing as `cruel and ludicrous`. "

The jailing also provoked a horrified response from members of Parliament.

John Hemming, the Liberal Democrat MP said:

"This is yet another example of how the secret family courts are stopping freedom of speech. I have never heard of a gagging order of this kind going on into adulthood.

This is a surreal case."

Mr Johnson`s local MP, John Baron told the media.

"I have helped Mr Johnson and his sons, who always wanted to live with him, over several years.

To find he has been imprisoned for sending a birthday message to one of them is troubling"

Adding:

"The family court system often ignores the legitimate wishes of families.

This needs to change, and quickly."

Sam Johnson told the media:

"My dad is a good father and has never been in trouble with the police.

He was treated like a criminal. This ludicrous gagging order should not exist and must be lifted.

Both Adam and myself are adults. This cruel ruling is now hanging over my father to silence him about the sons he loves for the rest of his life.

This is a terrible thing in what is meant to be a free country."

I became known all around the world and my story appeared in American, Australian and Canadian newspapers.

In the UK I appeared in The Daily Mail, The Times and The Sun.

I even got a mention in Mumsnet.

I was imprisoned a day before senior judges revealed they planned to stop courts jailing defendants in secret for contempt.

What was my contempt of court?

Here is the Facebook message:

"21 Today – 21 Today.

Happy Birthday Sam, love from Dad, Adam and Princess Lucy".

This meant without knowing I had breached a 6-year-old Gagging Order.

I received a letter in late April from Chelmsford County Court ordering me to attend Basildon Magistrates Court on May 2 for a hearing regarding my children.

I was not warned I might face imprisonment or that the hearing was about my Facebook message posted on Sam`s birthday a few days earlier on April 23rd.

On arrival, I was escorted by court security guards to a private room in the building for a half hour hearing under Family Court rules before His Honour Judge Damien Lochrane.

I sensed something was not right. There was no notice of the Hearing on the door.

It was a Magistrates Court but the room was empty.

No journalists, no members of the public and no court officials

I had no lawyer and was told the audio recording equipment was not working.

It was a secret hearing that resembled Nazi Germany or Soviet Russia.

I learned I`d breached a Gagging Order imposed by the Family Courts in 2007.

My ex-wife had reported me for wishing Sam "Happy Birthday".

The court overlooked the fact that both he and Adam had lived with me since 2005.

I saw them every day.

I was their Father. A single parent with sole custody.

It was perfectly legal for me to be both `mum and dad`.

I cooked their meals, washed their clothes and made their beds.

We watched TV and attended football matches together.

My love for both boys was unconditional as was there love for me.

34

We spoke every day in the privacy of our own home, in the street, over the park, but according to my ex-wife I must not wish them "Happy Birthday" on Social Media.

She reported my Facebook message to the court.

Judge Damian Lochrane said:

"Mr Johnson, you are not allowed to mention your children in public"

I replied:

"Are you saying I couldn't post a `Congratulations` advert in the local paper if they were to get engaged or married?"

He responded: "If you did that would be another contempt of court".

I informed the Judge I'd had three heart attacks and was awaiting a triple heart by-pass operation.

But he still sentenced me to 28 days in jail saying "prisons have hospitals"

They do, but not special Heart Units.

I was handcuffed and sent down to a underground cell to await transport to Chelmsford prison.

In the court cell I became ill and had another heart attack on my way to jail.

On arrival I was rushed from the prison to Chelmsford hospital by ambulance.

I was then shackled and handcuffed to a bed while on oxygen and receiving morphine.

A team of prison officers were put on 24-hour shifts beside my bed to make sure I did not escape.

There was also a guard on my door.

I was not a bank robber, a terrorist or high-profile East End gangster but a doting dad.

An innocent Father fighting for justice.

Months later I would have 2 triple heart by-pass operations, `die` twice and spend a month in a coma.

But when and how did this nightmare start?

It's a long story, but a bloody good one that involves everyone from politicians, the police, social workers, Underworld legends to Hollywood movie-makers.

At times although it reads like a cross between a soap opera and a horror movie it is 100 per cent factual.

A real-life drama with more twists and turns than a decade of EastEnders storylines.

I took my case to The High Court where a ruling by Lord Justice Munby meant I could legally tell my story.

The truth, the whole truth and nothing but the truth.

Everything in this book has been confirmed as 100% factual by the courts, Essex Police and the 500 plus legal and medical documents I obtained by using The Freedom of Information Act.

Highlights:

Forensic Psychiatrist Dr Sian Llewellyn Jones stated:

"Garry Johnson has a flamboyant personality, spiky hair, a marked Cockney accent, talks very fast, wears dark glasses and has a strange dress sense, but is not mentally ill".

So who is freedom fighter Garry Johnson?

He`s an East End boy who looks like Ray Winstone, talks like Danny Dyer, and dresses like Paul Weller.

He`s a punk in Mod clothes.

A David Bowie fanatic with a life-long addiction to blondes and always supporting the under-dog.

To quote Michael Caine, "not a lot of people know this" but underneath this rough, tough-looking exterior I`m a big softie.

I`m also smarter than I look. The public school educated professionals were in for one hell of a fight.

The custody battle would confirm what I already knew.

Posh middle-class people with Oxbridge accents are scum and the true enemy of the working class.

This wasn`t just a run-of-the-mill divorce and custody battle it was all-out class war.

You can say what you like about politicians, estate agents or even journalists, there are no bigger liars than social workers.

The most corrupt people in the UK are not coppers or criminals, they are Family Court solicitors.

My divorce was not a straight-forward split that ended with a friendly handshake.

It was more like a horror film with a cast of hundreds including politicians, gangsters, High Court Judges and a former boyfriend of Princess Diana.

It was not a normal separation.

My wife deserted her family for a man who wasn't nice, normal or single.

He was a former pimp, a self-confessed child abuser with a common-law wife and three kids.

Though that changed when his other-half found out about the affair.

She confessed that their eldest child wasn't his.

What is it they say?

"What goes round comes around".

They also say that `confession is good for the soul`.

Maybe it was catching.

A few days later the boyfriend admitted threatening and verbally sexually abusing my children to the police.

My ex-wife admitted in court that she did nothing to stop his vile behaviour.

This included an incident which angered the Judge but not Social Services.

Her boyfriend phoned my 12-year-old son and after threatening to beat him up with an iron bar boasted, "I am the man fucking your mum and your sister."

Adding:

"Lucy is in bed with us taking pictures. Do you want to see them?"

My daughter was just 5-years-old.

I then did something I had never done in my life. I contacted the police.

The cops went to pick-up Grimson and a Child Protection Officer interviewed my daughter.

She visited me the next morning saying:

"Mr Johnson we've spoken to Lucy and I can assure you she has not been physically hurt".

Adding:

"Mr Grimson has admitted making the phone call but claims he was drunk".

My divorce reads like an X-rated soap opera but believe me you are not reading a work of fiction.

I have the legal, Social Services and medical documents that prove every fact.

My story isn't based on a romance that went wrong it's the true account of a 15-year marriage and the 13-year divorce that followed.

The Freedom Fighter

My ex-wife accused me of being a `bad dad` and Social Services accused me of being everything from `mentally ill` to the Leader of a cult and would you believe a `Conservative Politician`.

As a life-long anti-establishment working-class rebel I took great offence at such a slur.

On one occasion a Judge in the Family Court claimed I was "more dangerous than a bag of heroin" when ruling I couldn't see my daughter.

This was minutes after I was accused of having the personality of a cult leader.

No evidence was ever produced to support such outrageous claims.

It took me 8 years of fighting a corrupt system to completely clear my name.

Before you read my story and learn about my fight for justice which ended in The High Court, via the Houses of Parliament and a high security prison.

Before I go into great detail please allow me to introduce myself to you and my daughter.

Four years ago I woke up in Basildon Hospital after 29 days in a coma following life-saving surgery at the hands of world famous heart surgeon Dr Hasnat Khan (Princess Diana`a paramour).

I thought I'd only been asleep for one night, when in fact I'd been unconscious for almost a month.

My heart stopped beating twice and my internal organs collapsed. My sons were who were at my bedside were told their dad may not make it through the night.

As you can see I made it.

I had to as `Dead men can`t talk` and I had a blockbuster of a story to tell.

But this is not even the start of it.

Let's rewind to the beginning and hopefully it will explain to my daughter why I fought so hard to be in her life.

When I was 13, my parents divorced and my dad walked out of the family home.

Social Services became involved in my life and I ended up in care.

That is when my hatred for Social Workers began.

Peter Brown was not my first middle-class mister know-it-all who became my enemy.

My hostility dates back to my childhood.

With him it was just another day at the office and I was the latest victim of his extreme prejudice.

Whereas with me it was both personal and historical.

It was all out `class war` where two cultures clashed.

In his eyes I was the lowest of the low.

A working-class cowboy with a Cockney accent and no intelligence.

It's true I didn't have his privileged background or University qualifications.

But was something he wasn't.

I was honest.

I was also a lifelong champion of the underdog and a `natural born fighter`.

It's part of my DNA.

My immediate hatred and distrust of him was both personal and historical.

No way was I letting the Gestapo wing of Essex County Council take Sam or Adam away from me.

Peter Brown was not aware of what or who he was taking on.

He'd soon find out I'd be no pushover and would become the biggest challenge of his career.

It would be a fight to the death with only one winner and no way was I going to lose.

I wasn't a typical dad who only saw his kids for a couple of hours every evening.

I was a house-husband. I worked from home.

Since day one of Fatherhood I'd been a primary carer and hand's on dad.

Dealing with babies was difficult.

Hard work and Julie did the lion`s share.

It only became a `piece of cake` after they`d had their Second birthdays.

It was hours of non-stop fun with every minute an absolute pleasure.

I was without being big-headed a `bloody great dad`. At last I`d found something I was really good at.

I didn`t care what the Family Court said I wasn't given up my dream job for the likes of Peter Brown.

I`d failed at everything else.

But I was born to be a dad.

I never made it as a footballer, boxer, pop star, punk singer, actor, stand-up comic.

I convinced myself I could sing like David Bowie with the attitude of Johnny Rotten.

I looked the part, but when I opened my mouth I sounded like an out-of-tune barrow boy.

I had a way with words and could write a good protest lyric but never really made it as a punk poet like Billy Bragg or Tim Wells.

I got lucky and sweet-talked my way into Fleet Street and somehow managed to have a career as a showbiz writer and TV critic.

But Fatherhood was what I was put on this earth for.

I took to it like a duck to water.

I was so good I think it scared Julie because in many ways I made her redundant.

I`m not talking about the practical stuff but when it came to love and affection, playing games, having a laugh, messing about it was all me.

I never said "no" to them and spoiled them rotten because it was a pleasure to do so.

It gave me a buzz.

The nicest thing my ex-wife ever said to me had nothing to do with sex or how I looked.

It was this:

She said:

"If I came home and told you the kids wanted a donkey in the back garden I know you`d say `yes` ".

It`s true I would have agreed instantly without a moment of hesitation.

I am so proud of my next statement. I will always consider it my greatest achievement.

I can honestly say I never hit my children, not even once and rarely told them off.

I left that kind of thing to Julie.

Not out of laziness but because I`ve always considered smacking a form of bullying.

I hate it when I see other parents hitting their kids in the supermarket or over the park.

I was the most easy-going liberal dad in the world. I was constantly attacked for this by Social Services and the Family Courts.

They accused me of treating my sons like friends.

They just didn't get it.

I had always treated both boys as mini-adults it wasn't something I did to score points after the divorce.

I was crucified for being too close to Sam and Adam.

Social Services even accused me of behaving like the leader of a cult.

It was total bollocks and said without any knowledge of my background.

I `lost` my parents and grew up in care. I did not grow-up in a secure and loving home. I didn`t have a home.

I spent my formative years sleeping on friend`s sofas, floors, in spare rooms and sleeping rough.

I wasn`t promiscuous as a teenager because I had no morals or wanted to be Rod Stewart.

I just wanted a bed for the night.

I decided on day one of the custody case that history would not repeat itself with my children.

I was one of the most hands-on dads in the world.

I was like a mum in Y-fronts but Social Services had no interest in the truth.

I must have done something right as years later both boys virtually lived in Basildon Hospital.

They were at my side throughout my coma and helped nurse me back to health.

I had no grip and couldn't use my hands so they fed me.

They held my drinks and made my phone calls.

Social Services would not have approved.

It was always my ambition to be a better dad than my own dad and I succeeded.

There was no way my ex-wife, Peter Brown or the perverted Richard Grimson would ever come between me and my own children.

It didn't matter how many draconian Court Orders or injunctions Judge Newton issued I would just keep on breaking them.

I would defy the authorities for as long as Sam and Adam wanted me to do so.

If they said dad "keep on fighting" then I was happy to keep on fighting.

I had an army of volunteers on permanent stand-by.

Whenever I was arrested, locked-up or hounded by the police they would give both boys sanctuary and a safe house to stay in.

These fantastic friends were more than willing to break the law for a good cause.

We saw ourselves as freedom fighters.

Modern day versions of the brave men and women of the French Resistance fighting against the Nazis.

Whatever the authorities threw at me it wasn't in my character to give in.

Surrender was never an option.

The stakes were far too high. You only get one childhood and one go at being a dad.

I was everything that Social Services and the Family Courts disliked.

I showed them no respect what-so-ever as is my world you have to earn respect.

It's not a god given right just because you're in a position of power.

Like my granddad taught me as a kid "you don't tug you're forelock to nobody".

I'd always be polite but I'd never cow-tow to bullies like Peter Brown.

I respected Lord Justice Munby and Judge Moloney on merit as both had something about them.

They were each a `class act` blessed with the common touch.

The High Court in London can be a daunting place. It's easy to be intimidated by people in wigs and gowns.

I wasn't just the plaintiff I was also representing myself against a highly paid barrister hired by Essex Social Services.

He could have `eaten me alive`. He expected it to be a `open and shut` case.

I was buzzing and prepared to be David to his Goliath.

I was expecting at best some kind of adjournment so I could live and fight another day.

Luckily for me the case was being heard by the formidable Lord Justice Munby.

He was either impressed or felt sorry for me standing alone against the legal team put together by Essex Social Services.

I was helped by the Judge almost every time I made a point or asked a question.

More on my victory later.

I knew from personal experience what it's like to lose a dad and have a terrible childhood.

I wasn't` going to rollover. I would not be another `pathetic` or `pushover parent` for Essex Social Services.

I'm sure when our conflict started they never imagined it would last twice as long as the Second World War.

I'd be the war hero Sir Winston Churchill to their mass murderer Adolf Hitler

Good against evil.

John Hemming MP and Alan Foskett the boy's solicitor both believe the case cost Essex County Council in excess of two million pounds.

The MP was so disgusted by my story he asked custody expert Jerry Lonsdale to work on my case.

The guy was a massive help and prepared my statement for The High Court.

I lost my liberty an sacrificed my health but would not hesitate to do it all over again.

I was just carrying out my duty as a parent.

I don't want to sound bigheaded but I'm proud of the fight I put up and the victory I achieved.

Peter Brown claims I'm the only parent who got the better of him.

It's quite something when you consider what he said at the start of our feud:

"I never Lose Mr Johnson".

I can confirm he lost.

I was the thorn in his side who would not go away.

My persistence, stubborn streak and fighting spirit broke him down.

I battered him with hundreds of emails and unwanted phone calls on a weekly basis.

I put two MPs on his case.

I grinded him into the ground and like all bullies he couldn`t take it.

The last I heard he was on `gardening leave`.

My `fight to the death` ended with me becoming a proud member of a very small and elite club.

I am one of only a hand-full people in the United Kingdom who has over-turned a Care Order.

Social Services declared war and it was a conflict I dare not lose.

Defeat was not an option. I had to win at all costs to stop history from repeating itself.

My dad ruined my childhood by walking out and it affected me all my adult life.

I found it hard to love as I feared being hurt. I believed those you love will always let you down.

I wasn`t wrong.

I can honestly say I`ve never let down the people I`ve truly loved.

I just couldn't do it.

It`s not in my DNA.

Like-wise it`s not in my character to forgive or forget.

I have never forgotten an act of betrayal.

An enemy is like a Christmas puppy. It`s for life.

That`s why I never truly forgave my dad and will never forgive my ex-wife.

In their own way they both betrayed innocent children.

I blamed him and always will for me not making it as a professional footballer.

I had natural skill and a god given gift but when he walked out it meant nothing.

I had trials with West Ham, Southend Utd, Leyton Orient and Queens Park Rangers.

Ipswich Town were also interested but was too young to travel the 70 miles on my own.

My dad`s new wife stopped him being involved in my football career so I quit.

I gave up a promising football career because of a `family bereavement`.

That is what it felt like at the time. The truth is my dad `pissed off` to be with the latest in a long line of fancy women.

I was broken-hearted.

I hung my football boots in the hope it would bring him home.

It was a big mistake and I should have carried on being the `Georgie Best of East London`.

I thought by turning my back on football I was getting back at him for `walking out` on me.

He had been a semi-professional with Brentford and played for Spurs Reserves.

It was always his ambition for me to play for West Ham United and thought wrongly `sod it`, I`ll show him.

It was a gross mis-judgement on my part.

He couldn`t care less and never came home. It`s hard to admit but my sacrifice was in vain.

The truth is my old man was a 100 per cent selfish bastard and never a doting dad.

He was more phony than Monopoly money and Tony Blair put together.

I worshipped him as a kid but hated him as an adult.

My ambition was to always be the opposite of him.

I wanted to be a proper family man, a great dad and faithful husband.

I like to think I was all three but still lost my wife and daughter.

I promised Sam and Adam I would never leave them and that they`d never have a stepmother.

I`m proud to say I have kept both promises

My low opinon of social workers and step parents dates back to my own childhood.

I did not speak to my stepmother for 12 years. We had a feud that lasted until the day she died.

It should have lasted longer, but in a vulnerable moment Julie got me to `kiss and make-up`.

It was a charade and not genuine.

We got a phone call in the middle of the night saying my dad had been rushed into hospital with a heart attack.

It was his wife and Julie answered on my behalf saying: "We`re on our way".

She could always persuade me to do anything.

It was a moment of weakness on my part and, as with Julie`s adultery, something I can never forgive.

I still beat myself up for agreeing to a truce.

This was the woman who talked my dad into leaving and then put me into care.

I visited but coming `face to face` with my stepmother brought back terrible memories of my unhappy childhood.

I immediately had flashbacks of incidents I`d tried hard to hide in the back of my mind.

I had never forgiven this woman for taking my dad and ruining my football career.

The day my dad left there was no explanation, no kiss goodbye or even a hug.

It was cold, brutal, heart-breaking, soul destroying and completely out-of-the-blue.

Deja-vu.

A carbon copy of when Julie left.

My dad and ex-wife had another thing in common. They both involved Social Services.

I was unlucky having a `selfish bastard` for a dad and bed-hopping blonde for a wife.

My hatred of step parents was nothing new. It was part of my DNA.

Richard Grimson was having nothing to do with my sons.

I did everything I could to keep him away from my daughter but my ex-wife had other ideas.

Julie teamed-up with Social Worker Peter Brown to help her build a new family.

She had recruited a very weak and willing `partner in crime`.

He was like a lovesick teenager and putty in her hands.

My friends would ask "is he giving her one or what?"

I`d reply:

"He`d like too, but I don`t think he is".

I honestly don`t think there was anything sexual between them.

The truth is Julie would have eaten the wimp for breakfast, dinner and tea.

He was just a star-struck social worker.

A male version of an airhead bimbo who hung on her every word.

If Julie told him the earth was flat and the moon made of cheese he would have agreed.

The trouble was this bumbling buffoon had so much power he was dangerous.

He was the Donald Trump of social workers.

I was `tipped off` by a `friend of a friend` that Julie and Peter Brown were monitoring my social media.

I was also warned about what I said on the phone as Social Services had the ability to hack.

I decided to flush them out and set a trap.

I posted a ridiculous message on Facebook that only an idiot would believe.

I claimed I was on day three of a hunger strike and Peter Brown believed it.

The next day I had an early morning visit from the Mr Bean of Social Workers.

"Hello Mr Johnson, we`ve been informed that you`re on hunger strike".

I laughed and said:

"Do what?"

He replied:

"We`ve been tipped off about your hunger strike."

I said:

"What you mean is you`ve been on Facebook".

I invited him into the dining room and on the table was my breakfast.

Slices of half-eaten marmite on toast, a mug of coffee, a Boost bar, a banana and an energy drink.

This was my normal breakfast.

Is it any wonder I ended up having 5 heart attacks and two triple heart bypass operations?

If Sam and Adam weren`t at school they could have confirmed the night before we shared Pizzas and garlic bread while watching the football.

Brown:

"Sorry, we were informed you was on hunger strike".

Me:

"By who?"

He grassed without hesitation saying:

"It was Mrs Johnson who told me to look at your Facebook page".

He added:

"I'd watch what you write from now on because Mrs Johnson monitors it."

I replied:

"And so do you".

He gave a sickly smile but refused to deny or confirm.

The dodgy `double act` were joined at the hip and also linked by not having any interest in facts.

They both thrived on half-truths, little white lies, manipulation and spreading malicious mis-information.

The odd couple invented fake news years before Donald Trump entered politics.

They were like Tony Blair and Alistair Campbell both experts in making false claims and producing dodgy dossiers.

Essex Social Services were happy for my daughter to live under the same roof as a self-confessed child abuser.

A friend of mine worked nights as a taxi driver and would see his car parked on the drive of 10 Carswell Gardens.

I'm pretty confident Lucy was too young to be aware of any of these facts.

It explains why I've been denied the right to be a father to my daughter.

My ex-wife was terrified of Lucy finding out the truth and why she doesn't see her dad.

That is why every time I went to court she objected to me having contact.

My daughter doesn't know between 2005 and 2013 that I applied to see her 23 times.

I also made more than a hundred requests to Social Services and direct to Peter Brown.

Is Lucy aware her mother took out Private Proceedings to put Sam and Adam into care?

She also started Private Proceedings to stop me having contact with my daughter?

Legal documents prove not once in 13 years did I ever ask the courts to stop my ex-wife from seeing Sam and Adam.

Julie also obtained various Court Orders forbidding me from putting any of the facts about the case into the public domain.

I was `gagged` but refused to be silenced. I spoke out and found myself in contempt of court more times than Tommy Robinson.

I went to court in Southend, Chelmsford, Romford, Basildon, Colchester, Cambridge and The High Court in London.

In desperation I contacted my MP and took my case to Parliament.

My pursuit of justice paid off and eventually I won permission to go public.

It was the effect of losing my own dad as a child that inspired me to fight on.

I never got over him walking out and knew from personal experience what Social Workers were really like.

Evil.

Pure evil.

If they`d lived in Nazi Germany they`d all volunteer to join the Gestapo.

If you don't believe me Google the names of young children murdered by step-parents while supposedly in the care of Social Services.

Maria Colwell, 1973.

Victoria Climbie, 2000.

Baby P, 2007

I wasn't willing to risk the lives of my children.

Social Workers have a well-documented history of having `blood on their hands`.

I recommend Googling `Children abused, groomed and gang raped in the United Kingdom`.

The vast majority were in the care of Social Services.

On their watch young children have been murdered and thousands of teenage girls` gang raped.

Media investigations and Government inquiries confirmed Social Services turned a blind eye and deaf ear to mass rape and child murder.

Thousands of young girls were groomed and raped by sex gangs in Rochdale, Oxford and Newcastle.

Investigations revealed Social Workers tampered with evidence and covered-up the abuse.

A top female police officer spoke-out and was forced to resign for telling the truth.

I grew up like a lot of working-class boys and teenage kids disliking the police.

I didn't know why it was just part of my Cockney culture and the influence of older boys.

My own sons have no dislike for the police but do share my passionate hatred for Social Workers.

They were threatened, bullied, harassed and mis-treated for eight years.

Essex Social Worker Peter Brown was a bully who tried to intimidate me.

He warned:

"You should stop fighting us Mr Johnson. You're wasting your time because we never lose.

I have never lost a case.

The Family Courts will always take the word of a social worker over that of a parent".

Adding:

"I can assure you Mr Johnson, you and your children will soon learn you don't take on Social Services.

The Judges always side with professionals and not the parents".

I'm not being big-headed, but this was the first time he had met someone like me.

He wasn't aware of my background and hadn't a clue about my personality.

Peter Brown was wet behind the ears.

Judge Moloney was a man of the world.

He was a true gent who recognised straightaway my British bulldog spirit and 'never say die' attitude.

The Judge told Essex Social Services:

"Mr Johnson won't just fade away and disappear. He is like a dog with a bone who will not give up".

Adding:

"If I was you I would try and work with him".

The Judge unlike Peter Brown was not gullible or a snob.

He did not look down on my thick Cockney accent.

The Judge was highly intelligent and worldly-wise who knew having a `thick Cockney accent` didn't equate with being `thick`.

Peter Brown and his high-command at Essex Social Services would soon find this out.

I didn't talk the way they all spoke but I wasn't stupid.

I was no ex-public schoolboy but `street smart` enough to hook up with two members of Parliament.

A top solicitor, The Sun, The Times and The Daily Mail.

I was also a life-long rebel who wasn't impressed by court orders, injunctions and `Gagging Orders`.

I would `fight to the death` to defeat them and keep custody of Sam and Adam.

I really was one of those who could walk the talk. I had a back story and a past that wouldn't allow me to lose.

Defeat was not an option.

Social Services were unaware of my dark secret.

They did not know about my own childhood of being in care and a victim of sexual abuse.

Abuse which was ignored by Social Services.

My hatred of perverts and Social Workers is historic and dates back to when I was a 13-year-old boy.

It started long before my own children were `violently threatened` and `verbally sexually abused`.

Decades before meeting Peter Brown.

That's why I was prepared to go to prison and risk my life to get justice.

In 2010 after five years of conflict I won the battle but not the war.

My case was no longer confined to the corrupt goings-on behind closed doors in secretive Family Courts.

I'd already been to parliament, appeared at The High Court and appeared on 2 radio shows.

Essex Police knew all about me as did the Leader of Essex County Council.

As with the police the closer you get to the top of an organisation the better you are treated.

Nicky O'Shaughnessy was the Head of Essex Social Services and a lady I must have driven nuts.

I bombarded her with phone calls, emails and letters on an almost daily basis.

She knew all about the Johnson family.

I wasn't shocked when she agreed to meet me as I'd given her a blow by blow account of my complaint.

If nothing else she had to be curious. It also helped that she'd received a letter from John Baron MP.

She wasn't aloof or cold.

I thought no way can this woman be a former social worker.

She was more like a record company press officer or TV researcher.

Nicky was well-mannered, polite, smiled and interested in what I had to say. This lady was nice and not a robot.

I told her so and she laughed.

We had the first of our many meetings in her plush office inside Chelmsford Town Hall.

The first time we met in person was a massive shock.

Nicky was not a stuck-up snob with a massive ego.

She was a real-life human being.

Blonde, chatty and friendly with a warm personality.

The opposite of Peter Brown and his motley mob of middle-class bullies.

She treated me like a paid-up member of the human race.

It was all very civil.

We shared a joke and I even made her laugh.

To quote Margaret Thatcher after her first meeting with President Gorbachov:

"I knew this was someone I could do business with".

I handed over a few letters and some documents which she promised to read.

This was the start of our peace negotiations.

We had a few more meetings where I turned on the charm and slaughtered Peter Brown.

Nicky than did the unexpected.

She completely wrong footed me.

I was lost for words.

She asked if I would introduce her to Sam and Adam saying:

"I've read and heard so much about them I'd really like to meet them in person".

Adding:

"Can I come to yours and meet them"?

I was stunned.

People like her at the top of a company rarely leave the comfort and safety of their ivory towers.

I was more shocked by what happened next.

A few days later the head of Essex Social Services was a guest in our house.

Peter Brown was at her side and this time more like a puppy dog than a Rottweiler.

Talk about `how the mighty fall`.

He was humble, silent, awkward and playing second fiddle to his boss.

Brown was like the school bully who`d just been beaten up by the new boy.

The three of us were expecting a visit but not a personal apology.

It was the first time she`d met either Sam or Adam but instantly connected with them.

Nicky O`Shaughnessy was unlike any member of her staff and everything Peter Brown was not.

A kind and caring human being. I thought surely there`s no way this woman was ever a member of the Essex Gestapo.

Nicky shook hands and cuddled both Sam and Adam saying:

"I`m sorry boys, I`m so sorry, I really am sorry but we don't always get it right".

The three of us chatted for about 45 minutes and before leaving she said:

"These boys are a credit to you Mr Johnson".

I`m a pretty good judge of character and this was no face-saving exercise or an act.

Nicky O`Shaughnessy was being 100 per cent sincere.

We now had a verbal aplology but just like Oliver Twist I wanted more.

This wasn't the final curtain. The game hadn`t ended. The war wasn`t over.

A moral victory maybe, but it would take three more years before I was granted an official inquiry and received a written apology.

Sam and Adam were a mission accomplished but I still had to fight on to see my daughter.

The Cockney Rebel

When my dad left I stopped playing football and became obsessed with David Bowie.

I became a life-long rebel which years later would help in the bitter war with my ex-wife and Social Services.

They could knock me down but such was my character I'd get straight back up again.

I was in pieces when my dad left but refused to cry or show any emotion, just as I didn't shed a tear when he died in 2010.

I never forget or forgave and never attended his funeral. I am many things, but I am not a hypocrite.

I am living proof that time is not always a great healer. Inside I was still hurting and maybe my daughter is hurt and angry because I wasn't part of her childhood.

It is something I regret every day of my life even though the facts prove it wasn't my fault.

Hand on heart if I was in any way to blame I'd say, "sorry Lucy" and walk away.

I mean that most sincerely.

If I had deserted my daughter. If I had abandoned her I would understand her decision to ignore me.

I would be too ashamed to show my face.

I would support her 100 per cent and respect her loyalty to her mum.

I think maybe be she doesn't want to see me because she'd feel disloyal to her mum.

I understand that. I respect that.

What if that loyalty is based on the lies?

That is not fair on Lucy or me.

You can't be loyal to a person who has wilfully fed you a diet of lies.

I didn't walk away and have spent the past 15 years doing everything to see my daughter.

I want to put the record straight before it's too late as dead men can't talk.

I know I was wrong to carry on the feud with my dad all the way to the grave.

The bitterness never went, it ate into me. I allowed it to enter my soul and that was wrong.

This is why I'm desperate to see my daughter before it's too late.

I want Lucy to know how I fought with every fibre in my being to see her.

There was nothing more I could have done.

My daughter has no genuine reason to hate me. The fact is she doesn't know me.

How can you dislike something or someone you don't know?

I would say only if you were brainwashed.

There is no other explanation.

I want my daughter to know I am not a 'bad dad', a 'terrible Father' or in any way mentally ill.

Consider the facts Lucy, if I was a 'horrible person' or really considered 'mad, bad and dangerous' by the authorities how did I get custody of your brothers?

Sam and Adam have lived with me since 2005.

No doubt your mum has told you I am 'anti-female' or don't like women.

This is the same lie she told Peter Brown, Social Services and the courts.

Your Mother had an agenda and on the advice of her solicitors lied to fit her narrative.

She was advised to paint as ugly a portrait as possible and portray me as being sexist and old-fashioned.

I became a bogey man figure and was branded a male chauvinist pig.

Her mission was to imply I was not a suitable person to bring up a little girl.

I have no idea how much my daughter can remember about me or of being five-years-old.

Please allow me to tell you as I have always had a photogenic memory.

Even before I became a showbiz journo.

I can remember everything about my own childhood, teenage years and virtually every detail of my marriage.

Sam and Adam will confirm my ability for total recall.

The truth is you was my `little Princess`, and a `Daddy`s Girl` who followed me everywhere.

I could not leave the house or go to the shops without you coming along.

Sunday nights you`d sit on my lap watching The Simpsons and I`d tell you bedtime stories.

I`d make up adventures about a big red bus full of animals that always landed on the moon.

It was your favorite story.

Before the divorce we were like Ant & Dec. We were a double act.

You were my shadow. We were rarely apart. If you can`t remember.

Don`t take my word for it. Check with people who knew us as father and daughter.

`Aunty Emmy` the lovely Irish lady who taught you at St Gabriel`s playschool.

I often chat to her in Pitsea High Street.

Sara Reynolds, the nice blonde woman from your playschool in Shotgate.

They will both confirm it was me who collected you most days.

I was the one who turned up with either your bike or pushchair.

You can trust Aunty Emmy her daughter Angela Smith was the Labour MP for Basildon.

I met her last year at a Jeremy Corbyn rally in Pitsea and put my foot right in it.

I joked it was about time Labour abolished the Upper House.

Why is that funny?

Angela now sits as a Dame in The House of Lords.

Aunty Emmy always asks about you, Sam and Adam. As does Sarah who last month became a grandmother.

The truth is before the divorce your brothers were already known as `The Johnson Boys`.

They were one hundred per cent `Daddy`s Boys`.

Your mum was not happy about you being a `Daddy`s Girl` and in her mind joining the `Garry Gang`.

That is what she called us.

This is not me having a pop at your mum but a fact of life.

Children have always liked me because I'm not a boring old stuffy adult.

I was a bit of a Pied Piper.

Our house was always full of kids. Sam and Adam could invite whoever they wanted.

Sometimes your mum would come home and there'd be dozens of them running about all over the house.

She'd say "It's like a bloody youth club in here."

If you don't believe me ask your brothers.

Or visit any of the 'old neighbours' at 30 The Gables Pitsea and 64 Chestnut Road Pitsea.

I always believed in an open house policy.

Packed with kids during the day and full of adults in the evening.

I liked to be surrounded by people.

I'm telling you this to prove I have never been 'mentally ill' or 'mad, bad or dangerous'.

I liked nothing more than hearing laughter and seeing people having fun.

At 64 Chestnut Road I set up a snooker table in the dining room, table tennis table in the conservatory, and a full-size football goal in the front garden.

I also turned the garage into a games room with a massive TV and Play-station for Sam & Adam.

Ask anyone if your dad was always the "life and soul of the party".

I admit sometimes even the most normal of situations got out of control.

I was about 21 and the family all went up North to stay at my mum's big house for Christmas.

Ten of us went to the pub on Xmas Eve but only nine returned.

I met this girl and without going into details didn't return until Boxing Day.

That was how I lived my life.

It wasn't planned things just happened to me. From managing The Stone Roses to writing a Hollywood movie.

That's how I coped with being banged-up in a high security prison and being told I'd never be released.

I'm a survivor.

There is only thing I couldn't have coped with. It would have destroyed me.

It scares me even thinking about it.

It's a situation than even with all my survival instincts and the 'luck of the Irish' would not have survived to fight another day.

I would not have come up smelling of roses.

I often wonder what if Julie had left me for a really nice bloke who loved my children.

And worse they loved him.

It would have been like a 'stake through my heart'. It would have 'killed me' and probably led to his murder.

There is no way some bloke would play 'dad' to my children.

As they say "Every cloud has a silver lining".

My ex-wife had her pick of any man in the world but chose a self-confessed child abuser.

I knew he would never be there dad.

It was a blessing in disguise.

Maybe there is a God.

I've always been a person who attracts people.

In normal circumstances none of this would be of any interest to anyone or my daughter.

It only becomes important when you've been falsely accused of being some kind of 'headcase'.

I'm just trying to show I am nothing like the person I've been branded.

I've been subjected to a hatchet job that the Russian Secret Services would be proud of.

I want my daughter to start asking questions.

What happened when we attended parties as new people to the area.

Who did all the talking?

Was it your mum or dad that hooked-up with 'new friends'?

Ask about the night I took over the Karaoke machine in a house full of strangers.

We arrived late and only knew the hosts. I immediately went into mingle mode.

They loved my Cockney punk impressions of Tom Jones and Elvis Presley.

There`s a video which shows your mum hiding at the back of the crowd.

She was scared I`d get her to do a duet. Our party piece was a version of Sonny & Cher`s, "I Got You Babe".

None of this would be important unless I was trying to show my daughter she has a false impression of me.

I am what`s known as a `people person` who has always loved to have fun.

I never took life seriously before I got involved in a custody battle.

I want my daughter to ask her mum if I always loyal.

Confirm or deny that wherever we went between 1989 and 2004 I always told your mum afterwards:

"You were the best-looking one there".

It wasn't flannel as I genuinely meant it.

We were at a party full of West Ham footballers, TV stars, pop singers and page 3 girls like Linda Lusardi, Sam Fox and my favorite Suzanne Mitzi.

I would love my daughter to ask her mum about that night at The Stratford Apollo.

It was full of lovely ladies but in my eye`s Julie was the best.

She had no problem with me chatting to all the blonde models or the good-looking gay guy flirting with me.

The same came not be said about her reaction to Antonella.

She was a stunning model the tabloid press dubbed "the black Marilyn Monroe" who I`d known for years.

Your mum always had a problem with me and black girls.

I bumped into Patsy Johnson another old friend down Walthamstow Market.

We hugged and kissed after she`d gone your mum slapped me round the face.

Look her in the eye and mention the black girl with dreadlocks.

I`ve always had a thing about blondes and black girls.

The perfect woman is Rita Ora a beautiful black lady with blonde hair.

As was David Bowie`s ex-lover Ava Cherry.

A question for my daughter.

Has your Granddad, my former father-in-law still got a `problem` with black people?

Do you know his sister married a black guy and he never spoke to her again?

Your mum has mixed-race cousins she was never allowed to meet.

If you go on Facebook you will see pictures of me and my best mate from school.

The two of us as teenagers and in 2017 hanging out at The Estuary.

The best Gluten Free diner and bar in Southend-on-Sea.

Were pictured in Central London with Talk Radio star James Whale and partying with model Zoe Anderson at The Circus Tavern.

I mention this because Vere is a black guy with dreadlocks which I hope explains why I never got on with your Grandad.

He is/was a bigot.

You know I`m telling the truth.

I can only imagine the comments you were subjected to growing up.

He hated blacks, Jews, Muslims, homosexuals, The Labour Party, the Daily Mirror and what he called "biased BBC news reports".

Lucy. Have I painted an accurate picture of Mr Taylor?

As Sam and Adam got older I`d say to your mum "Please tell him to stop mouthing off in front of the boys".

The only thing we ever agreed about was that night followed day.

Though to wind him up I`d say "day followed night".

I don`t know if your mum does this with you, but because of her background as a dental nurse she had a thing about teeth.

Whenever we left anywhere the first thing she`d say on the drive home was:

"Do you see that person`s gunky teeth?"

Your mum had an obsession with dental hygiene and was always flossing.

She`d trap Sam, Adam or me in the bathroom and wouldn't let us out until she`d flossed.

The funny thing is and I`ll never understand how this happened.

It confused me and your brothers.

Despite her obsession with having nice teeth her boyfriend had most of his front teeth missing.

I`m not joking and he was also bald. I don`t mean shaved like a gangster.

I`m talking hereditary.

He was bald as in losing his hair with a beer-gut and no personality.

Your mum could have had anyone (and probably did) but walked out on her family to be with a Shrek lookalike

A former pimp and self-confessed child abuser but what is the old saying? "Love is blind".

The truth is my ex-wife wasn`t just scared about me meeting Lucy she was terrified.

And with very good reason.

Julie knows my character better than most and knew Lucy would `love me too bits`.

That is why she couldn`t allow it to happen.

The truth is Sam, Adam and Lucy always thought the world of me and the feeling was mutual.

This didn't just make my wife an unhappy bunny it made her insecure.

I have no idea what she`s like now but throughout our marriage she was a very jealous person.

I often got a whack around the head for looking at other women.

I stress `looking` as I only ever looked.

It was not her fault but a `personality trait she inherited from her mother.

Julie did have a weird relationship with both her parents.

It`s hard to explain but she was scared of them. NOT in a physical way as I don`t believe they ever hit her as a child or teenager.

She was just a completely different person in their company.

They molly-coddled and treated her as if she was still a child rather than a grown-up.

A wife and mother.

She always acted weird around them. The only time we kissed in front of them was on our wedding day.

Julie couldn`t show any emotion and would tell me not to talk about `certain subjects` in their presence.

I`m a very tactile person and so was Julie when her parents were not around.

She was always all over me and forever kissing and cuddling the children.

Your mum would be affectionate in front of other people but never in front of her mum and dad.

If I went to kiss her she'd flinch and pull away. I don't mean in the weeks before she left I'm talking about the 15 years we were married.

What would a psychiatrist make of this? Does this explain why she had such a high sex drive and was an animal in the bedroom?

I was lucky that I married a woman who was like a female version of me. No she didn't have a big nose or a thick Cockney accent.

Some people are hooked on drugs, others alcohol, gambling or both, but luckily for me, my wife was addicted to sex.

She was, to quote the Buzzcocks song, "an orgasm addict" and for 15 years I was more than happy to feed her addiction.

I don't know what my daughter is like or how she has grown-up but pray to God she's more of a Johnson than a Taylor.

No that is unfair. I'll re-phrase that.

I hope my daughter is more like her mum, the Julie I 'loved and lost' than her grandparents.

I hope she is fun and likes to have a laugh. A bit of a liberal who tries to see good in everyone.

In Julie's defence moving down the pecking order must have been hard to accept.

She was the love of my life, but such is my character I find it hard to have more than one special thing in my life.

To begin with, it was always Julie first, second and third.

Then it became Sam and Julie, then Sam, Adam and Julie, and eventually Sam, Adam, Lucy than Julie.

I couldn't multi-task when it came to affections which is another reason why I couldn't have an affair. I would have been the world's worst ever adulterer.

I suppose without intending to I pushed her away. It wasn't deliberate, but the truth is, you can't break a habit of a lifetime.

I can only handle one obsession at a time and my children replaced Julie as the most important things in my life.

It was a no contest.

I still loved 'Julie to bits' but I worshipped my three children more.

I suppose becoming a doting dad 'trumped' the role of being a loving husband.

Sam and Adam were `Daddys Boys` from day one.

My ex-wife was horrified as every day Lucy became more and more of a `daddy`s Girl`.

She was my `Little Princess`.

My mother-in-law would make half-joking/snide comments about how `Lucy was getting just like the boys and following Garry everywhere`.

She knew how to press Julie`s buttons.

The truth is I wanted a normal and civilised divorce.

Not true.

I promised to be 100 per cent honest so I will be.

I didn't want any kind of divorce.

I don't believe in marriage or divorce.

In a perfect world the five of us would have stayed together forever but that wasn`t possible.

My ex-wife had a new boyfriend and that was the choice of her and her mother.

If there had to be a split I wanted it to be amicable.

There is no way I would have involved solicitors and social services.

I do need people telling me what to do or advice from strangers.

I will ask my daughter to read all the documents and see that despite pressure from my solicitors I refused to say anything bad about your mum.

Please check and you`ll see what I said.

This is a direct quote:

"Julie was always a good mum who would never hurt her children" adding "that is why I can`t understand why she refuses to condemn the behavior of her boyfriend".

And the Judge agreed. I`m know I`m repeating myself but it`s true "Love is blind".

Your mum had fallen in love with a self-confessed child abuser".

Another old saying is also relevant.

"Opposites attract".

Their relationship was a classic `beauty and the beast`.

As mentioned earlier about 8 months before Julie left I was suffering with stress and early signs of my heart problems.

I was put on medication that lowered my sex drive and drove her into the arms of others.

The first time before the tablets `kicked in` I couldn`t rise to the occasion Julie was not pleased.

She was naked and `gagging` for it. She called me every name under the sun and how can I put it `finished the job herself`.

Julie thought wrongly that I`d gone off her.

Her constant cravings and daily demand for sex eventually destroyed our marriage.

What if it had been the other way around?

If Julie had gone off sex for a while would I have cheated?

I can honestly say "No". I would have waited until she got better.

I would not have risked losing Sam, Adam and Lucy.

My ex-wife was without question a sex addict so maybe, and giving her the benefit of the doubt, perhaps her two affairs were partly my fault.

Julie needed her fix and when I couldn't supply her `drug` of choice she looked for another supplier.

I always try to grab a positive from a negative situation.

So, was it better to of been married to a sex addict for 15 years then not to have been married to her at all?

I couldn`t even be a flash bastard and say "it was me who had Julie in her prime" because every time I saw her in court she always looked stunning.

More blonde, more sexy and somehow younger.

If I couldn`t see my daughter every day I wanted to her every other day.

That was refused.

As was seeing her every weekend. My ex-wife refused any contact what so ever.

The documents prove that between 2005 and 2008 I only saw my daughter 3 times.

The venue was Willowbrook Contact centre with each meeting lasting an hour.

I was treated like a criminal and chaperoned by you`ve guessed it social worker Peter Brown.

I was given a list of what I could and couldn`t talk about.

I was warned the visit would end if I asked a question he didn`t like.

My bag was searched as were the presents I brought along for my daughter.

Was the Barbie Doll sexist?

What did they think I was hiding inside the packets of sweets and cans of Cola?

Were there hidden messages inside the comics?

How many politicians or middle-class people know or even care how working-class dads are treated?

This another reason why I`ve written this book.

I want to prove how the United Kingdom is not a democratic country.

It`s a Third World dictatorship which treats innocent people like convicted criminals.

All contact was stopped after 3 meetings.

My ex-wife refused to bring my daughter along and Social Services stood by and did nothing.

I was told "If Mrs Johnson won`t bring Lucy there is nothing we can do".

I have not seen my daughter for 10 years.

What is it the ruling class say "British justice is the best in the world".

I hope you don't mind if I politely disagree.

My ex-wife couldn't accept having to share our daughter.

She was advised her best option for exclusive rights was to smear and destroy my reputation.

I was accused of planning `serial murder` of being `mentally ill` and a "pornographer".

The picture she painted of me was a million miles from the truth.

Fake news.

Blatant lies.

Slander.

It was so vile and vindictive it was obvious that Julie was being advised what to say.

She didn't possess such a hateful streak or creative imagination to concoct such a tissue of lies.

Julie could not have been so evil acting alone.

My daughter deserves to know the truth and my ex-wife reminded of it.

Here come the facts.

I am without doubt one of the most `female friendly` men you`ll ever meet.

I`ve got both a track record and back story to prove it. I can walk the talk.

I have always admired strong, smart and independent women all my life.

I always wanted an older sister. I always wanted a daughter of my own.

I joked when Lucy was born. I repeat it was a joke because years later my ex-wife told Social Services that I meant it.

I`ll say again for the avoidance of any doubt, it was a joke.

I said:

"Lucy will wear braces on her teeth and have a crewcut until she`s 18."

Adding:

"because I know what boys are like."

I didn't mean it and Julie knew it was just the kind of thing I`d say.

It was an innocent joke.

I also said something like:

"Now I`ve got a daughter were moving to a desert island because I know what boys are like".

At the time everyone thought it was funny and was me just being me.

Fast forward five years.

Julie told social worker Peter Brown: "If Garry sees Lucy he`s threatened to shave her hair off".

She claimed Lucy would be in danger and that I was planning to kidnap her.

These lies became part of the Social Services narrative used against me.

They were repeated by my ex-wife behind the closed doors of the fascist Family Courts.

My daughter must read the hundreds of legal documents now in my possession.

She could also make a Freedom of Information request for her own copies from Essex Social Services.

Lucy would not have to go to court as nowadays you can apply online.

I was according to Peter Brown a danger to my ex-wife and 3 children.

I'd heard all this rubbish before but then he pulled a rabbit out of the hat.

I was also a danger to myself.

Julie and Peter Brown painted this bizarre picture of me as a serial Killer in waiting.

A soon-to-be mass murderer with a death wish.

I was suddenly a suicide risk who was a danger to children and hated women.

It was like being in an episode of Prime Suspect.

The truth is I genuinely love the female of the species

I've always loved women and don't mean in just a crude sexual way.

I find them better company than men as I love to gossip.

The conversation is always more fun and entertaining.

I'd always choose to be stuck in a lift or on a desert Island with a woman.

I'd rather go for a drink or a meal with a woman.

I shared so many enjoyable 3-hour inter-city train journeys with female press officers.

There was never a dull or silent moment.

I love to talk, I was born to talk which is why I had such a 'love affair' with fast drugs.

The more white-lines I snorted the more I talked.

I'm not sure if Julie will admit the following, probably not, but throughout our marriage she'd say:

"The minute you wake-up you start talking."

Adding:

"Before your feet even touch the ground you're already starting a conversation."

We all have annoying character traits and I admit that was one of mine.

My ex-wife also had annoying habits. We had 2 toilets at Chestnut Road but she'd still come in the bathroom and have a 'wee' when I was shaving.

It always bugged me.

The truth is I have always loved the company of women and as a teenager longed for an older sister.

After Sam and Adam were born all I wanted was a daughter to complete the family.

My dream was for her to be a journalist like Rebekah Wade (Brooks).

I think women are the superior sex. They are certainly the most loyal, caring and kind.

You know the saying `Don't judge a book by its cover`, well that applies to me.

I look like tough guy actor Ray Winstone and talk like Danny Dyer`, but have a massive feminine side to my character.

I say to my daughter.

Ask you mum the following question. Look her in the eye and ask `Did you always call my dad camp`?

Julie mocked my showbiz-style mannerisms and the way I talked with my hands.

It was the Cockney/Jewish part of my character combined with my love of the theatrical.

That's why I`ve always got on with gay people and think Julian Clary is a funny comedian.

Graham Norton a brilliant chat show host and Ziggy Stardust the greatest rock star of all-time.

I truth is I am the least male chauvinist person you will ever meet in your life.

If you don't believe me do the following.

Log onto Facebook and direct message the list of people I am going to name.

I am sure they will confirm what I`m about to say.

In a very particular order:

Rebekah Wade (Brooks) was my boss for 16 years.

She was also the first person to ring when I got out of Bellmarsh prison.

The lady is a diamond.

She also sent a massive Fortnum & Mason hamper when I returned home from Hospital.

My daughter`s middle name is `Rebekah` which I hope confirms my admiration.

She is the great plutonic `love of my life` and one of the most loyal people I`ve ever met.

A class act in every way.

As a tribute the smart, sassy, classy, sharp journo in my novel Serial Killer is called Rebekah Woods.

Annette Witheridge was my boss at The Daily Star. Now based in New York but still in touch.

Sharon Marshall was my boss at The Sunday People and rewarded me with my own soap opera column.

She is now the TV pundit on This Morning with Phil Schofield and Holly Willoughby.

I also supplied stories to Jane Moore (Loose Women) and Claudia Connell at The Sun.

My top media contacts were Joanna Burns, Patsy Johnson, Jasmine Kimera, Chrissie Cremora, Jenny Torring, Bernadette Coyle and Erica Echenberg.

My oldest friends who knew me long before my ex-wife are Leigh-Anne Franklin and Toni King.

They all have two things in common they are not men and are all `females of the species`.

As are my publisher Teddie Dahlin and the producer of my film Sandie West.

And there is more.

The volunteers who helped when Sam and Adam were on the run from Social Services and hiding from the police were all female.

I could not have coped without the help of Justine, Diane, Sarah, Kelly, Jodie, Karen, Samantha.

These women don`t like me for my looks. I should know as I see myself in the mirror every morning.

It`s because I`m `female friendly`.

I`m not being big-headed, well maybe a bit, but I know my daughter would love me.

It is why her mum did everything in her power to stop us from meeting.

She was terrified of having to share our daughter.

This is a bit like a job interview.

I`m trying to sell myself to Lucy.

I am not and have never been mentally ill, a manic depressive or `god forbid` boring company.

If we meet there is no way I`d hurt, depress or bore you to death.

I`d have you laughing within minutes.

I want the job of being your dad.

Give me the chance to prove it.

I`m a nice guy. I am also funny. Ask your brothers and their mates.

They film me watching TV and making outrageous comments.

I am according to them more entertaining than watching C4`s Gogglebox.

They can`t all be wrong can they Lucy?

Showbiz journalist Garry Bushell has interviewed all the comedy greats in his career but always calls me "the funniest bloke he`s ever met".

I did 2 shows with TV funnyman Phil Jupitas last year.

A lovely bloke, we got on like a house on fire and he called me "a very funny fella."

That is some compliment coming from a top professional comedian.

The was a team captain on Never Mind The Buzzcocks for 10 years.

He`s worked with all the comedy greats like Ricky Gervais, Jimmy Carr, Frank Skinner, Lee Mack, Rob Brydon.

Can you imagine how chuffed I was when he said I was funny?

We hung out together for hours and I wasn`t even drinking so must be good company.

I`m not showing off or bragging for the sake of it.

It`s to show my daughter I`m not the person she`s been brought up to believe I am.

I`m doing my best to sell myself to someone who considers me a bad person and her enemy.

I want my daughter to know the real me which is why in this book `I pull no punches`.

If she doesn`t like what she reads or the person I really am, I can live with that.

My daughter will be judging me on the truth and not a pack of lies.

If we do get to meet I promise her 2 things.

I will not do a comedy routine or say anything horrible about her mother.

I`m so desperate to see Lucy she could even bring her mum along.

There is nothing I wouldn`t do for a chance of us being reunited.

I`m talking about with my daughter, not my wife lol.

On the day I probably wouldn`t be able to even talk.

I`d be a right mess grinning from ear to ear and crying like a baby at the same time.

Can you do both at the same time?

Let us find out together.

Paul Wellings now there is a name from the past.

He is the he husband of your mum`s friend Lisa and no fan of mine but checkout his book `I`m A Journalist Get Me Out of Here`.

I think it`s a fiver on Amazon. I`ll buy you a copy.

He claims and I quote word for word:

"Garry Johnson is the funniest bloke I`ve ever met."

So aren`t you interested in meeting me and judging for yourself?

I want my daughter to be like those women Davina McCall meets on ITV`s `Long Lost Family`.

To stop being a teenage version of Meghan Markle.

I am at heart an eternal optimist and `old-fashioned romantic` who still believes there could be a happy ending.

I wish there`d been a Hollywood style fairytale ending with my dad.

Sadly, that ship has sailed. You can`t turn back time.

I often wonder what might have been.

I don't want history repeating itself and the same thing happening to my daughter.

It would be a tragedy.

My daughter might not think it now but could live to regret it.

I didn't make up with my dad and the only person I`ve hurt is myself.

It doesn`t affect him because he`s dead.

Not burying the hatchet was a mistake and not saying "goodbye" is something I regret but can`t change.

Maybe if he`d written a book.

A letter saying "sorry" for ruining my childhood there might have been a happy ending.

Like `ifs and buts and monkey nuts` wasting time on `what might have been` is a negative use of energy.

Life is all about the future and moving on.

So, we move on.

I want my daughter to know the real Garry Johnson.

The man who is her biological dad.

I mention that term because a social worker once had the cheek to ask if Lucy was my `flesh and blood`?

Did he go to the same charm school as Boris Johnson?

I admit I`m a Cockney rebel who all his life has broken and bent the rules.

A working-class liberal who embraces the modern world and the culture of anything goes.

I can`t stand middle-class traditions and old-fashioned conservative values.

Except when it comes to family.

Then I become like a Jacob Rees-Mogg character in a period drama.

I believe in love and marriage and the content of a Mills and Boon novel.

I become the perfect English gentleman who believes in old-fashioned British values.

A loving husband and doting dad.

A man deeply in love with his wife and extremely proud of his children.

What I`m trying to say is the Married me was nothing like the single version.

As a single person I cheated all the time.

Most people do, but as a married man I was one hundred per cent faithful throughout my 15-year marriage.

That`s the gospel truth, cross my heart and hope to die.

I swear that on my life.

And when you`re living on borrowed time that had better be true.

That doesn't make me a hero.

It`s not hard being faithful when you genuinely love your wife and believe in your wedding vows.

It also helps when your wife has the face of Patsy Kensit and the body of Amanda Holden.

I was never Saint Garry.

I just knew where my bread was buttered and, what`s that old saying?

"Why eat beef-burgers when you`ve got steak at home?"

Though that didn`t apply to me because I was a veggie I still agreed with the sentiment.

Using another relevant analogy I think it was Jerry Hall who said a man wants `a goddess in the kitchen and a whore in the bedroom`.

Julie was both.

She was also the love of my life and mother of my children so being unfaithful never crossed my mind.

My ex-wife was an out and out animal in the bedroom with the sex drive of a high-class call girl.

So now you know why part of me still misses her.

Bollocks to the bravado.

I don`t just miss her body, I miss her mind, sense of humor and smell.

Though to be honest I think most guys would miss her.

My old man had a roving eye and wandering hands but once I got married I became a one-woman man.

There is no way I would have risked losing my family by having a one-night-stand or a fling.

Well here goes.

One last throw of the dice and a bit of a gamble.

I`m relying on the honesty of someone in the enemy camp and the ability of my daughter to decide if she`s being told the truth or a lie.

Fingers-crossed Lucy is a good judge of character.

I want my daughter to question her mum`s sister.

Ask Sharon Williams.

The only member of the Taylor family I genuinely liked and I think it was mutual.

Though she wouldn't say that lol.

If she didn't genuinely like me I can only say she was a bloody good actress.

Maybe it`s in the genes because Julie gave award-winning performances in films like `Saturday Night Specials` and `Basildon Babe`.

I only met Sharon 20 times at most because she lived in Wales but we always got on.

Julie was the beauty of the family and she was the brains.

I genuinely liked her even though she beat me at Trivial Pursuit and Who Wants To Be A Millionaire.

Sharon was a member of MENSA and went to University so no shame in losing to her.

I would have her roaring with laughter and she`d have me in stitches with her dry and acid wit.

Go on Lucy.

See who blinks.

Dare Sharon to let you look her in the eye and ask the question face to face

Stare directly into her eyes and ask: "was my dad funny?"

If she says, "no he wasn`t" I trust your judgement to see through a lie.

I am 100 per cent confident that she won`t be able to deceive you.

A part of me even thinks she might have the decency to tell the truth.

Some background information about your dad which proves that in one way or another I`ve always been a bit of a performer.

I have never been dull, boring, mentally ill, middle of the road or stuck in a rut.

I hate doing nothing or sitting still.

I don`t do sun-bathing and always like to be on the move.

Ask your mum.

I don`t like silence. As soon as I wake-up I put on the radio in one room, the TV in another and have to play my music.

Ask your mother.

I always talked through Television shows which drove your mum nuts.

She claimed I fidgeted at the movies and sung too loud at concerts.

I was many things but I was never `down`. The glass was always half-full and never half-empty.

My ex-wife under the influence of a person I compare to Ian Huntley, and worse my daughter was living under the same roof as a monster.

Nobody seemed to care that Richard Grimson had sick sexual fantasies about my daughter and bragged about them to my eldest son.

Since walking out Julie had stopped me from seeing Lucy and separated brothers from sister.

In the past 13 years I have only seen Lucy for a grand total of 180 minutes.

That's three one-hour meetings in 2008 at The Willowbrook Contact Centre in Basildon.

The venue is cold, bleak and sterile.

All three meetings were held under the strict supervision of Social Services security guards.

Each with the personality and charisma of a Gestapo officer.

I was convinced that one day they would make me wear a concentration camp style suit and brand me with a number.

I was treated like a Jew in 1930s Germany or a black man in apartheid South Africa.

My sons last saw Lucy in 2007 at the same secure contact centre.

They had to go through a number of locked doors and were told what they could and couldn't say to their own sister.

Do politicians have any idea what is going in the United Kingdom?

My son was told he couldn't talk to his own sister at school.

It shocked me and should shock and out-rage all decent people.

Adam attended Hilltop Junior School and Lucy went to the Infants.

They were in separate buildings but shared a playground.

Adam and Lucy were spotted talking at playtime and separated by a teacher.

They were pulled apart and I'm told both children got distressed.

I was phoned by the Head teacher and told "Please tell Adam he must not have any contact with his sister".

When I asked why.

I was told "We've had instructions from Mrs Johnson to keep them apart."

This decision received the full backing of social worker Peter Brown.

I was told by the Family Courts that if I went to the media I'd be in contempt of Court.

Adam soon moved to his senior school so that was the last time he spoke to his sister.

Do people reading this book now understand why I hate Social Services?

Has the author always had a raging social conscience and dislike of authority?

Was Peter Brown his first encounter with a bully?

Jerry Harris writes:

"GARRY JOHNSON was the first and best of Britain's street-punk poets.

A former Borstal Boy, his 'Boys of the Empire' collection brought poetry to a whole generation of working class punks and skinheads.

East Londoner Gal articulated the frustrations felt by a million teens trapped in Maggie's dole-queue Britain of the early eighties.

The Business were the first of many punk bands to set his raw, heart-felt and angry poems to music.

When Street-Punk was crucified and libeled by all sections of the British media, Garry Johnson's vision helped to keep the new movement together.

He was radical, anti-racist and anti-establishment. His message was: black and white working class youth have the same enemy and the same interests.

Class was all that mattered to Garry.

That is why he fought back when the upper middle-class legal system and middle-class social workers declared war on him.

His poems were about life at the bottom. His natural enemy were the Tory party, but Garry also attacked the middle-class drop-outs playing at revolution and the gentrification of the Labour Party in poems like 'Suburban Rebels' and 'Labour MPs Ain't Working Class'.

He was anti-New Labour even before Tony Blair invented it and took the UK into illegal wars.

Garry went on to manage The Stone Roses, he blagged his way into journalism, Essex Social Services persecuted him for a hellish period, he was thrown into high security Bellmarsh prison for defending his children against a self-confessed child abuser.

A verdict that defies logic, sense and natural justice.

Garry Johnson has had an extraordinary life with more twists and turns than a decade of EastEnders".

Talking to Paul Hallam of Streetsounds magazine:

"All my life I've been a contender who never quite made it.

But I never gave up."

Adding:

"That is why I was the perfect person to take on Social Services and the corrupt Family Court system.

Every time they knocked me down I got straight back up again.

I kept going because I knew I had right on my side.

The authorities did everything to silence me but at The High Court in London Lord Justice Munby ruled against Essex Social Services and removed the `Gagging Order`.

He told the barrister representing Essex Social Services:

"You can appeal against my verdict but I will not change my mind".

The floodgates were now open and shortly afterwards Judge Moloney ordered Essex Social Services to handover all the secret files.

Those documents and others I obtained by using the Freedom of Information Act made this book possible.

Before becoming a `seeker of truth and justice` Garry was best known as a punk poet.

He tells Essex Life magazine:

"I started writing poems because I couldn't sing in tune."

Garry talks fast, maybe because he doesn't think he has long left.

He jokes:

"Dead men can`t talk.

That`s why I`m writing this book now and want to get it all down before it`s too late."

A few years ago the Punk Poet came close to writing his last lines and saying his final words.

He had a Triple-Heart Bypass that went wrong and spent 29 days in a coma and on a life support machine.

Twice his children were told `prepare for the worst` as he clung onto life and battled with septicemia.

His life was saved by world renowned Heart surgeon Professor Hasnat Khan, the former boyfriend of Diana, the Princess of Wales, who inserted a metal valve to save our working class hero.

With his heart working at only 30 per cent capacity and a guarantee of only five more years, Garry wants to put his story into the public domain.

He says:

"The specialists told me `most of your internal organs are damaged and not fit for purpose`.

Sadly they can't do anymore for my heart, liver and damaged kidney".

Adding:

"Time is running out and if I don't get to tell my daughter the truth in person at least she can read all about it when she's older.

I just want her to know how much I loved her and how I always fought to see her".

The odds were massively stacked against me.

I want my daughter to know I was a lone wolf.

A solo voice fighting against a choir of corruption.

It was me against her mother, grandparents, Social Services, Cafcass, a biased Family Court and a corrupt team of lawyers.

I took inspiration from The Hillsborough families and parents of Stephen Lawrence.

Like them I would not take no for an answer.

If my daughter doubts a single word of this book or extracts taken from interviews.

The solution is easy.

Ask your parents to take a Lie Detector test. Talk to your brothers or read the official documents.

At the end of the day the truth can't hurt you. Knowing the facts can only educate you.

Contact Wickford police and Essex Social Services. Talk to your mother about the vile and perverted behavior of her boyfriend.

Fact.

When I write I always apply the 'Domino Effect'.

The rules being that even if you tell one little 'white lie' and get found out it weakens the credibility of anything else you might have to say.

I would not take the risk.

This story is far too important to even consider telling a single 'white lie'.

In this book every sentence of every paragraph in every chapter is for better or worse "the truth the whole truth and nothing but the truth".

I want my daughter to know the real Garry Johnson not some cleaned-up and sanitised version.

I refuse to go down the same road as Tony Blair and Alastair Campbell.

They are perfect examples that if you produce a dodgy document you will always get found out. The lies come back and bite you on the bottom.

Blair destroyed his reputation by lying and I want to restore mine by telling the truth.

What would be the point of me lying?

I don't think Lucy would be impressed.

If I got found it would give her the perfect excuse to keep on ignoring me.

She would quite rightly feel betrayed. I would lose any chance of gaining her trust.

Once trust has gone it can never be restored.

The stakes are far too high for me to risk lying and losing my daughter forever.

Love Marriage Divorce

After the divorce, our two boys chose to live with me, following a series of rows with their mother over her new boyfriend Richard Grimson.

But within a year of the divorce, my ex-wife made false allegations to Essex Social Services.

She claimed I was neglecting my children and not feeding them properly.

An investigation by social services cleared me of any wrongdoing and confirmed both boys were fine.

I never doubted the outcome for one minute.

They trained at a professional football club and followed a healthy diet recommended by fitness trainers and sporting nutritionists.

A year later my ex-wife made further false allegations to social services claiming I was mentally unfit to care for the boys.

I was examined by a local psychiatrist who was personally appointed by social services.

They expected him to support their position.

He didn't.

The psychiatrist examined me and wrote to social services saying:

"There is no evidence of mental illness. I cannot understand why there are concerns about Mr Johnson's mental health."

A disappointed Essex Social Services had to call off their dogs of war.

But Peter Brown would soon be out of his kennel.

More false allegations followed.

Mrs Johnson informed The RSPCA I was neglecting pets.

They turned up on my doorstep accusing me of not feeding my cat.

I did not own a cat. The boys did not own a cat. There was no cat living at 22 Bridge Road.

The following week 2 council officers turned up accusing me of fly-tipping rubbish in my own back garden.

They looked and there was no rubbish.

It then went from the silly to the serious.

Two guys in suits and ties with matching briefcases turned up on my doorstep.

They were from the Benefits Department of the Government and accusing me of fraud.

I had nothing to hide so invited them in.

The Nazi with thick-rimmed glasses and the Gestapo attitude sneered:

"Mr Johnson we believe you are claiming child benefit for two children"

He was shocked when I replied "Yeah that's right".

I explained that as both Sam and Adam lived with me I was entitled.

He called me a liar saying:

"but your sons do not live with you Mr Johnson".

I replied:

"says who?"

His colleague chipped in with "their mother".

My ex-wife had reported me for fraud.

I started laughing and this gave them the right hump.

The guy in the cheap suit and second-hand spectacles said:

"Do you think it's funny swindling money out of the government Mr Johnson?

You can go to prison for fraud".

I replied:

"I didn't know that really, thank you very much for letting me know".

They thought they had me banged to rights and wanted to interview me under caution.

I said:

"Slow down a bit boy's, let's not get ahead of ourselves".

I offered them a tour of the house.

Starting with the boys' bedrooms with wardrobes full of clothes, football kit and school uniform.

Posters on the wall and toys on the floor.

Bikes in the garage, and a 5-a-side football goals in the back garden.

The `Little Hitler`s` weren`t so cocky now but wanted more proof.

It was against their training manual to believe I was telling the truth.

I immediately rung the school who confirmed both Sam & Adam lived with me.

According to the Government guys from the DSS they`d been contacted by my ex-wife who`d told them Sam and Adam were living with her.

She would make similar allegations on two more occasions.

I was more baffled than angry.

Why was my ex-wife harassing me with false allegations?

She was the guilty party who`d run off with a self-confessed child abuser.

Although her lies were annoying they were not life-threatening or life-changing.

That would soon change.

Her next attempt of character assassination involved pornographic films.

This time I was smeared at Southend Magistrates Court.

My ex-wife alleged I made adult movies.

It was a smear too far that spectacularly backfired. But a smear she`d return to again and again.

Why did Julie put our private and personal life into the public domain?

Her aim was to embarrass and destroy my character in the eyes of Social Services.

Was I the first male victim of revenge porn?

What she was thinking?

Those advising her thought it was clever but it was not a smart move.

It`s one thing ringing up The RSPCA , The Environmental Health Department and the DSS.

Making a serious allegation on oath in open court is taking it to another level.

It`s also pretty stupid unless you want the world to know you starred in porn films.

Why would she want that information put into the public domain?

No way was I going to stay silent and let Social Services think I was some kind of pervert.

I had no alternative but to exercise my right of reply and clear my name.

Now was time for the truth, the whole truth and nothing but the truth.

I admitted to making around 30-plus pornographic films between 1992-2004.

I felt like a black man at a KKK rally. I was without doubt the most unpopular man in the courtroom.

The disapproving looks on the faces of all those present said it all.

They were all looking at me as if I was some kind of dirty old man in a plastic raincoat.

Though to be fair to them they had no idea of the content.

They soon would.

My ex-wife had me on the ropes but hadn`t landed a fatal knockout blow.

I glanced across the room at a smug looking Julie who was thinking to herself `I`ve got him this time`.

She hadn`t.

The blood drained from her face when I was asked to elaborate.

"What kind of films Mr Johnson?"

I replied in the best cheeky cockney manner I could:

"Good honest porn Sir, nothing more nothing less. There was nothing dodgy or perverted. Just your everyday porn.

I should know because I wrote the scripts. I also filmed and directed all the movies".

Adding:

We started doing them in 1992 and continued for about another 12 years"

I was asked to explain what I meant by "we".

So, I explained;

"Me and Julie.

Sorry, I mean Mrs Johnson and myself. Julie was the star and we made about films

We made the last one in the summer of 2004"

I wasn't proud of talking about it in public, but what choice did I have?

I was fighting for custody of my sons.

The court and social services had to know I wasn't some kind of pervert which was obviously Julie's intention.

Why else would she bring the subject up?

I could only defend myself by revealing content of the films and got away with revealing as little detail as possible.

Julie wore wigs, sexy Santa outfits, naughty nurse uniforms and dressed up as St Trinian schoolgirl.

I was told "Thank you Mr Johnson we've heard enough."

So didn't have to mention her Anne Summers dressing-up box, collection of sex toy or the fur hand-cuffs.

The truth is as the facts and court papers prove I was a victim of revenge porn.

I was 'outed' as an adult movie-maker.

It was Julie who put her porn films into the public domain in a desperate attempt to make me look bad in the eyes of Social Services.

Her illogical attempt at smearing me backfired.

Had she used her brain instead of the hatred in her heart our Saturday night specials would have remained a secret.

Most of her behavior that day was completely irrational and obviously not thought out in advance.

Not only did Julie 'out' herself as a porn star she requested the return of 4 films and 59 pornographic pictures.

It gets more bizarre.

She even told the Judge I'd brought some of the video films to court. Why on earth would I do that?

Was I planning to sell signed copies?

I was told to hand my bag to the usher and I watched it being searched.

It contained a comb, a mobile phone, hair gel, Jaffa Cakes, bottle of Lucozade, a picture of my 3 children, copies of The Sun and Daily Mirror.

No pornographic films or photographs of Julie were found.

What was it with Julie and her obsession with bringing up her porno?

Why embarrass herself to try and get at me?

It didn't make any sense and she certainly wasn't 'once bitten and twice shy'.

At different times Julie would repeat slight variations of the same porn allegations to the police, Social Services and Cafcass.

Always without producing a shred of evidence.

Julie lied to Social Services.

She claimed I'd sent naked pictures to her boss but failed to produce them.

We are led to believe he threw them in the bin.

She told Peter Brown I'd sent pornographic photographs of her to 22 Bridge Road.

And would you believe?

Lucy opened the letter saw the pictures of her mum and burst into tears.

I ask again, do you believe that?

Peter Brown did.

Important question.

Did Julie hand the pictures over to Peter Brown, the police, social services, her solicitor or Cafcass?

No.

We are meant to believe she destroyed the `photos` by tearing them up and throwing in a bin.

Now my name is not Sherlock Holmes.

I never attended the Police Training College at Hendon but even I know you don't destroy vital evidence.

It's just a suggestion.

Just putting it out there for discussion, but maybe Julie was lying.

What do you think?

What was it my solicitor said when I was found "Not guilty" of posting clips of her porn career on the Internet?

"Mr Johnson did nothing wrong.

He is the innocent victim of what can only be described as malicious slurs".

So once again I'd cleared my name and retained custody of my sons.

It didn't stop her campaign of false allegations.

My ex-wife started private care proceedings to remove the boys from my care.

It was a Family Court Hearing so once again no evidence was required.

All Julie had to do was wear a figure-hugging dress and flutter her eyelashes.

It was a `no contest` as Peter Brown and Cafcass supported her application.

It was a done deal.

I knew how Family Courts operated. It`s all done with smoke and mirrors.

They rely on `paper referrals` written by so-called experts you never meet.

Dodgy dossiers and biased reports based on the allegations of Mrs Johnson (whether they`ve been proved or not).

The opinion of Peter Brown, the suggestions of Mrs Johnson`s Legal Team and the documents from ex-Parte Hearings you weren`t allowed to attend.

The decisions made at those secret Hearings are never removed from the paperwork.

They are written in stone and follow you around like a bad smell.

At a secret Hearing in 2006 I was falsely accused of being `mentally ill`.

I was cleared in 2007 and again in 2008 but it took 4 years before Social Services accepted I was not `mad, bad or dangerous.

Then another 3 years before I got a written apology.

The Judge ordered that both boys should immediately be removed from my care but the ruling wasn`t worth the piece of paper it was written on. Sam and Adam were not impressed and like me blatantly ignored it.

The next morning Peter Brown knocked on the door and they weren`t in, well not to him anyway.

They would spend the next 6 months on-the-run and staying at safe houses all over Essex.

At times it was like being in a movie.

The boys would sneak into the back of a motor and hide under a blanket.

They`d be taken to a supermarket or Railway car park and be transferred to another waiting motor.

I think they found it quite exciting.

They were driven across County lines and put up in a house just yards from the Eastenders studio.

Life imitating art.

They stayed at 5 different locations in Wickford.

A safe house on Canvey Island and various places at Southend, Laindon, Grays and South London.

They eventually just came home and why not?

They weren't the Kray Twins with every cop in the country looking for them.

It was just Peter Brown with his silly bit of paper.

The Court Order was like a nine-bob note.

Worthless.

Brown knew they were living with me (Julie told him) but without the police could do nothing.

Social Services were powerless to act. Two schoolboys were giving them the run-around and they didn't like it.

My ex-wife and Peter Brown joined forces and took me back to court.

I was ordered to hand the boys over. I refused.

I was told I had to persuade them to give up.

I refused and was threatened with prison.

I still refused.

It was a game of brinkmanship. Who would blink first?

I was supposedly given one last chance.

The court ordered that I hand Sam and Adam over the next morning.

It was never going to happen. It didn't.

Peter Brown arrived with the police and what a surprise both boys were out.

My ex-wife suspected they were hiding at the homes of Diane Prior and Justine Salmon.

They were.

I'm not dropping them in it or betraying a confidence as you'll discover when you read on.

Those names are a very important part of my story and I want you to remember them.

Diane Prior and Justine Salmon.

They both received a summons through the post to appear in court.

Please remember the names.

Justine and Diane were both told by a Judge not to allow either boy into their homes.

They were served with court orders warning them of the consequences.

If Sam or Adam entered their houses they would be arrested for 'contempt of court'.

I hope you haven't forgotten the names.

A few weeks later the police picked-up both boys in the local park.

They were issued with a police document which stated both boys could legally live at the home of Justine Salmon.

The police officially announced they would no longer be involved in the case.

My ex-wife went ballistic when she found out.

What could she do without the police?

You've guessed.

Is it a bird, is it a plane? Is it Superman?

No, it's Peter Brown.

What could he do without the police to do his dirty work?

He visited Justine and agreed both boys could legally stay at her house.

The bully boy had no choice lol.

This was fine at first and we celebrated our great victory with a meal.

There was ten of us sitting around the table mocking Peter Brown and toasting the police.

I had social services on the ropes but like Oliver Twist I wanted more.

I visited Mr Brown in his Brentwood office with a very short list of demands.

I wanted my boy's home.

I wanted Sam and Adam's Care Orders revoked.

I wanted the Private Proceedings halted and contact with my daughter.

Peter Brown started calling me "Garry" instead of "Mr Johnson.

We both knew he was losing control. The days of him trying to intimidate me were over.

He claimed:

"I can't get the Care Orders revoked".

Adding:

"That just doesn't happen".

I replied:

"I want it to happen".

He rambled on about how I should be happy because the boys were no longer wanted by the police and living legally with Justine.

Adding:

"There 5 minutes from your house and we both know what`s going to happen.

How long will it be before there back at yours"?

I tried not to laugh thinking maybe he`s not as stupid as he looks.

I was wrong.

He was still pretty pathetic saying:

"It`s me who has got to face Mrs Johnson and she`s not going to be very happy".

He was right about that.

My ex-wife bombarded him with new and old allegations about my mental health.

I met him again and asked if there was any news about my list of demands.

Would the boys be coming home?

When will they be living with me legally?

He rambled on and on and on about it not being possible and how Mrs Johnson wouldn`t allow it.

I wondered out loud if my ex-wife was now in charge of Essex Social Services?

Brown replied:

"Mrs Johnson is still saying your mentally ill. I want your help to get her off my back".

He added:

"If you help me I promise to help you"

Brown wanted me to see a Forensic Psychiatrist saying:

"If you get the all clear I`ll recommend that both boys can live with you".

Was it really an offer I couldn`t refuse?

My legal advisers and both MPs advised I take him up on his offer.

I agreed on condition I got his offer in writing.

It was forthcoming in less than 24 hours.

The hospital I attended in East London was more like a prison than a medical centre.

It was like an inner-city version of Broadmoor.

There was a high wall, bars on the windows and locked doors at every entrance.

When I commented on the building to Dr Sian Llewellyn-Jones revealed:

"I usually deal with murderers and serial killers".

Had I been set-up by Peter Brown?

I said to myself:

"Jesus, the bastard has set the bar pretty high".

My MP believes it cost Essex Social Services in the region of £7,000 to hire the services of Dr Sian Llewellyn-Jones.

So, what did they get for their money?

A nine-page report which gave me a `clean bill of health`.

I bet they was gutted when they read it. It was not what they hoped or were expecting.

So, what was her verdict?

"Mr Johnson has spiky hair, a friendly smile, wears dark glasses and has odd dress sense.

He speaks very fast in a marked Cockney accent. He has an expansive character and big personality.

He is a little eccentric but not mentally ill".

Apart from the comment about my clothes I thought she was spot-on.

The top Forensic Psychiatrist had virtually agreed with Dr Black , Joe Delaney CMHT, Dr Best and the shrink at Bellmarsh prison.

Had Essex County Council wasted £7,000 of tax payer`s money on a report that wasn`t necessary?

Here is the biggest shock Peter Brown kept his promise.

Social Services went back to court and the boys were put on a `living at home with parent` care order.

I`m told these Court Orders are like gold-dust and very rarely granted.

Sam and Adam legally lived with me and once or twice a month a social worker would call in.

They soon stopped coming.

Unbeknown to me I was still prevented from mentioning my case in public.

Even naming my sons in the most innocuous circumstances, such as Facebook, became a contempt of court.

The care order on Sam expired on his 18th birthday, or so I thought.

I believed the one on Adam would also expire on his 18th birthday.

Normally a `gagging order` imposed on a parent expires at the same time as a care order on the child.

This one did not which explains why my case was held in secret and behind closed doors.

Let`s go back in time as I don`t want you to forget how hard I fought for justice.

It was a marathon and not a sprint.

Do you remember the names Diane Prior and Justin Salmon?

They are both a very important part of my story.

I want to illustrate how by defying the Family Courts you can put Social Services on the backfoot.

You can cause confusion and contradiction.

That`s why earlier I said remember the names of Justine Salmon and Diane Prior.

The Courts said both boys were not allowed into their homes and threatened Justine and Diane with arrest.

They could go to prison for contempt of court.

Are you following this?

When I was sent to prison Social Services signed form confirming Sam and Adam could legally stay at the home of Sara Reynolds.

And you guessed it Justine Salmon and Diane Prior.

How can you go so quickly from `public enemy number one ` to `hero of the hour`?

It proves that Social Services and the Family Courts make it up as they go along.

And how do they get away with it?

They are answerable to nobody and all decisions are taken in secret.

I discovered it`s only the police who record interviews and they give you a copy of the tape.

Social Services and Cafcass refused every request to record our meetings.

I only obtained copies of documents because I went to court and won a freedom of Information request.

I was arrested, locked-up in a top security prison and told I would never be released.

My ex-wife had been advised to lie to the police and told them I was planning to become a serial killer.

According to her I was going on a murder spree.

She, her boyfriend and parents were on a hit list that included my solicitor.

Her allegation was one hundred per cent fiction as was a novel I`d written, but the police bought it.

Seven coppers turned up at my house and arrested me for threatening to kill my ex-wife and planning to carry out 5 murders.

I had not seen my wife or spoken to her for over a year so how was that possible?

According to her I`d changed my name to `Harry Harris`, a fictional character who lived inside the covers of a book.

If that`s sounds far-fetched so does being accused of being a serial killer.

Harry Harris was `guilty` of killing a pervert. He put three bullets in his head and then doused him in petrol.

But only in a book.

He killed one person so why was I accused of being a Serial Killer?

The victim was a fat bald man with no hair and no front teeth.

How was that a threat to my ex-wife who was slim, with long blonde hair and perfect teeth?

What was the connection?

I wrote a novel called Till Death Us Do Part using the alias of Garry Jackson.

I used a pen-name because I didn't want to `wash my dirty linen in public`.

Checkout Amazon and read the reviews which my prove my honesty and the publication date.

It was published 12 months before my arrest as a would-be serial killer.

Till Death Us Do Part was a work of fiction based on fact but in real-life Richard Grimson was not slaughtered on the streets of Wickford.

He was living in Wisbech and avoiding justice.

My ex-wife as films like `Saturday Night Specials` prove was a great actress.

She must have given the performance of her life to convince the police I was about to become a mass murderer.

I was arrested in front of my eldest son, handcuffed and bundled into a police van.

On my arrival at Basildon police station I am treated like Public Enemy Number One.

I'm surrounded by cops and medical staff from the Criminal Mental Health Unit who inform me I am 'mad' and a 'danger to society'.

Apparently I have 'mental problems' which is news to me, but they do say you learn something new every day, but I was not convinced.

It was like something from 'One Flew Over The Cuckoo Nest' with me in the Jack Nicholson role.

My clothes were taken away and I was given one of those white boiler suits you see on News At Ten.

I was interviewed by the white coat brigade for about 90 minutes then banged up in a freezing cold windowless cell.

A few hours later I'm taken by three burly cops for a cosy chat in a tiny intimidating tomb.

Another room without a view and no windows which was both claustrophobic and hostile.

I didn't have a clue what was going on or why I'd been arrested, but it soon becomes crystal clear.

I had been set-up by my ex-wife, her parents and boyfriend.

They read me a statement from Julie which is so full of lies, hate and spite it's was hard to believe we'd been married for 15 years.

I kept thinking to myself "she committed adultery, she walked out on the children, so why is she acting like a woman scorned?

None of it made any sense.

My arrest.

The pure hatred of my ex-wife and the allegations I was about to commit mass murder.

Two plain-clothed detectives enter the room, a moronic male and a very pretty female of the species.

Mister Plod was Fred Flinstone without the loincloth and it soon becomes clear that Lady Cop models herself on Helen Mirren in Prime Suspect.

I am face to face with a caveman cop and a wannabee Charlie's Angel.

They tried to engage me in conversation but for over an hour I stuck to "no comment" and amused myself by imagining the female cop in a black Baby Doll nightie.

`Fred` lacked the wit and charm of a Burtons dummy and she lacked the brains to go with her good looks.

We are talking `Dumb and Dumber`.

She was dead cute but he was brain dead.

Cutie played good cop and Fred acted the heavy, but I wasn't that impressed with their performances.

To be honest he was more Keystone Cop than Jack Regan and she was nothing more than a pretty face.

God help us if there ever asked to investigate a genuine crime.

The odd couple couldn't separate fact from fiction.

They couldn't work out that I was Garry Johnson and not East End gangster Harry Harris.

For over an hour on the advice of my brief I said nothing but "No comment" to every question.

But as the questions got more and more bizarre I couldn't remain silent any longer.

I tried to explain Till Death Us Do Part was a novel and that Richard Grimson wasn't really dead.

I asked have you read the book?

It was hard to understand why I was under arrest for writing a novel.

They said "Mrs Johnson claims you have a Hit List`.

I replied:

"No, the Harry Harris character in `Till Death Us Do Part` has a Hit List.

I am not Harry Harris.

I am not a gangster".

The truth is they didn't land a glove on me. There was no knockout punch and I won every round on points.

I wasn't expecting the verdict.

It was like a FIFA World Cup venue selection hosted by Sepp Blater.

Corrupt.

The contest was rigged and the result was fixed. The cops had all the power and were both judge and jury.

They had no interest in the truth or in believing my innocence.

To them I was just another working-class criminal.

If I'd been middle class with a posh accent I would not have been arrested.

I would not be sitting in a cell and being interrogated.

My brief said 'you've been set up' but assured me I'd soon be back home with my children.

Then against any form of natural justice I was charged, refused bail and remanded in custody for 2 weeks.

I was then told "you're looking at a life sentence".

The only thing I was guilty of was writing a novel. The last person sent to prison for writing a book was Oscar Wilde.

I was in good company.

He wrote The Ballad of Reading Jail so I re-wrote my punk poem 'Ballad of the Young Offenders'.

Oscar Wilde had Irish blood and like me was a victim of the British establishment.

I was 100 per cent innocent but with no connections to the House of Lords innocence means nothing

The young single mum who couldn't afford a TV licence or the OAP who didn't pay his Council Tax are in prison.

Tony Blair is a free man despite the media calling him a "War criminal".

I found myself handcuffed and locked in a windowless van bound for Bellmarsh Maximum Security prison in South East London.

Home to some of the hardest prisoners in the UK, including top gangsters, terrorists and murderers.

The cell inside the prison van was half the size of a phone box and felt like an upfront coffin.

Although I was going to a Maximum security prison I couldn't wait to get there as three days banged up in police station was torture.

It was just so boring, a tiny cell with no windows, 72 hours without TV, radio, newspapers or knowing what was happening to my children.

Were they safe?

At the time I knew I was innocent but not the victim of a stitch-up by my ex-wife and her family.

I thought she'd just lied to the police, but soon found out she'd been planning it for weeks.

She had formed an unholy alliance with the police, Social Services, a psychiatrist and the Criminal Mental Health Team.

I must admit It was a perfectly executed smear.

My ex-wife had tried previously tried and this time she enrolled the help of her boyfriend, fascist family and best friend `Ginger`.

And she almost pulled off the perfect scam but as they say "the truth will always come out".

Arriving at Bellmarsh which is London`s toughest prison was a bit like being in a film so I mentally transformed myself into the Ray Winstone character in Sexy Beast.

Winstone is one of my favourite actors.

Whenever I pile on the pounds people say I`m his spitting image, so when this book becomes a movie I want the great man to play me.

As I get out of the van there are helicopters buzzing around overhead.

I`m surrounded by a posse of masked men some carrying loaded guns and others failing to control barking dogs.

The reception area is deliberately daunting and I immediately thought back to Ronnie Krays funeral when Reggie arrived flanked by the biggest screws in the prison service to make him look small.

There were big burly bruisers everywhere.

Growling giants, dog ugly tubs of lard with bulging beer-guts, flat noses and cauliflower ears giving it large.

This is the screws I`m talking about, not the convicts.

They looked like an ugly combination of pit bull terriers and bar room bullies wearing Gestapo-style uniforms.

Intimidation was the `name of the game`, but to be honest, they weren`t that convincing or genuine experts in the art of menace.

These guys were nothing like Underworld legend Dave Courtney or boxer Mike Tyson.

All they had was strength in numbers and felt safe with odds at Twenty to One in their favour.

All cowards by nature and in reality the sort of fat kids who were bullied or ignored at school.

This was there playground and they loved the power of the uniform.

Away from the prison jungle they ruled with threats, intimidation and a book of rules they would dare not say `boo to a goose`.

But here they could play the big man and walk with a swagger, but in reality they were nothing more than two-bob traffic wardens in different uniforms.

A motley mob of second-rate SS stormtroopers with the brains of lollypop men and the attitude of fascist dictators.

I wasn't scared. I wasn't impressed. I had met many real genuine hard men from the world of boxing and London's underworld.

I'm not being big-headed or brave after the event because to be honest I was just too tired to be intimidated.

Three days in isolation away from my kids without food, drink or sleep had drained me.

Then for the first time in 72 hours I met my first genuine human being, a lovely old nun with the compassion of Mother Theresa and the warmth of Lady Diana.

A screw waived a piece of paper in front of me and asked:

"Are you mad? It says here you're mentally ill and suffer with Bipolar Disorder"

So I started frothing at the mouth and bite him.

Only joking.

But when I replied; "so they say"

I was separated from the other inmates before Walt Disney could hum 'Loony Tune' and put in a cage.

I felt like one of the Monkeys in London Zoo.

This was happening in modern day England. The home of democracy and a so-called civilised country.

I'd committed no crime yet here I was staring at a life sentence.

Being locked-up and losing your freedom is a punishment when your guilty.

But when you're innocent you're the latest in a long line of British miscarriages of justice.

The Guildford Four, George Davis, Colin Stagg, Barry George were all pardoned and released from prison after spending a total of 41 years behind bars.

How long would I be a member of that club?

The nun in the Mary Poppins costume and a sympathetic screw took my details and booked me in.

After 15 minutes of pacing up and down and singing to myself 'Anarchy In The UK' to lift my spirits.

I was given a cheap bottle of orange, a bruised apple and felt like asking "What no banana?".

When the door opened I was surrounded by three burly screws wearing army-style headgear and para-military body armor.

I was taken to a high-security special unit.

A prison within a prison.

After what seemed like a mini-marathon we stopped at another set of security doors and I was handed over to three more screws.

They were more my size and had the ability to walk and talk at the same time.

Not that well, but it was a vast improvement on caveman grunts.

The Neanderthals had left the building. Was this the Elite Squad?

I felt like one of those Jewish activists I had seen on TV in the 80`s being handed over to the Americans by the KGB.

We did another half-marathon and went in and out half a dozen steel doors.

The place had more locks than Fort Knox, no wonder Bellmarsh is escape proof.

All the time I`m thinking to myself "in a minute they will kick the shit out of me", but they didn`t.

Maybe I had a friendly face or did they really believe I was mad, bad and dangerous?

The Hannibal Lector of Essex.

I found myself in the special unit. A prison within a prison and home to genuine loonies and psychopaths.

I would spend the next 10 days in a windowless room isolated from the outside world.

As with my Three day incarceration at Basildon Police Station once again I had no idea about the whereabouts or safety of my children.

I felt like a `political prisoner` and was being treated as if I was `Public Enemy Number One`.

All I`d done was write a book exposing the pervert who had carried out a violent and sexually abusive campaign of terror against my children.

It was like a citizen`s arrest. A public exposure but it wasnt a crime.

It was justice.

I did the right thing but was banged-up in a top security prison and he got off with a caution.

The authorities objected and my ex-wife took offence because I executed her boyfriend in a novel.

Nick Love's movie 'Outlaw' was a vigilante film along the same lines as 'Till Death Us Do Part', but it wasn't banned and the producer hasn't been arrested.

At the same time as Sean Bean was promoting it on TV I was facing a life sentence.

It was almost Midnight when I was taken to a single cell about Twelve feet long and 6 feet wide containing a bed, a desk and a toilet.

This was no weekend break at a Butlins Holiday Camp and Ronnie Barker was nowhere to be seen.

I ate my apple and sipped from my bottle of cheapo orange juice trying to get my head around my situation.

Nothing added up.

I'd written a book, a revenge novel where my wife's lover got three bullets pumped into his fat ugly head for threatening my children.

It was a work of fiction that most decent people would consider it a fair punishment.

Julie was in the opposing camp and infatuated with the former pimp she reported his 'murder' to the police.

I sat in my cell facing life behind bars and wishing I'd done it for real.

I'll be honest with you, if I'm ever diagnosed with cancer I will kill the bastard.

That is a fact.

The day before I'm due to die I'll pump three bullets into him.

A bullet for each of my children.

I'd douse him in petrol and enjoy watching him go up in flames.

I've always been a working class liberal.

It doesn't make me mad, just a devoted Dad who wants justice for his three children.

I would only do it if I had a medically confirmed death sentence and genuine "get out of jail free" card.

This is because prison is nothing like the way it's portrayed in the movies.

It`s a hell hole full of losers. Not just bad guys but mostly sad people.

It`s not politically correct but do take my hat off to the chaps, the `proper people` surviving and able to smile in such shitty places.

The career criminals doing long stretches for being gangsters or robbing banks who have to live side by side with the dregs of society.

Low-life burglars, bullies, child-abusers, rapists, shoplifters and muggers.

It may not be PC or acceptable to middle-class professionals living the good life in Suburbia, but I`ve always been fascinated by charismatic criminals.

Real-life or fictional.

Al Capone, Jessie James, The Kray Twins, Ned Kelly and The Great Train Robbers.

Underworld legends and faces like Joey Pyle, Bruce Reynolds, Dave Courtney, John McVicar and crime families like The Adams & The Hunts.

I`ve read all the books and watched all the TV documentaries and grew up thinking of these people as modern day `Robin Hoods`.

I know that`s not true but they still fascinate me.

These were violent and ruthless men but lived by a strong moral code.

Their mantra was "you never harm women or children".

I`ve met a few and know they`d be shocked and appalled by the crimes committed against my children.

One of the chaps.

A top-of-the-range gangster and `friend of a friend` personally told me of his outrage.

The three of us visited his London mansion and he patted my youngest son on the head saying:

"Don`t worry your dad has told me everything".

Adding:

"I`m a dad myself, you leave it to me".

I got a phone call the following evening informing me "we`re five minutes from Wickford".

I`ll return to this later but will never reveal the identity of our knight in shining armour.

I won't name him but will give my honest impression of Bellmarsh Maximum security prison.

It's a powder keg waiting to blow-up.

It's a human dustbin, grey, bleak, noisy with a hostile and sterile environment.

I can honestly say prison is a shit-hole and a place where every day seems like a month.

I only did two weeks.

It was long enough to convince me how mentally strong people like Reggie Kray really were.

The East End gangster did Thirty-three years with great dignity without becoming bitter and twisted.

They tried but couldn't break him.

I'd always believed in the death penalty for monsters and child killers like Ian Huntley and Ian Brady.

Prison changed my mind and I'm now 100 per cent against state murder.

A full life tariff is a far harsher punishment then swinging from a rope.

If it was up to me all rapists, child abusers and members of grooming gangs would all get a minimum of 30 years with no parole.

I would let them all rot in a living hell.

In prison the cells are bare, cold and tiny, the atmosphere is hostile and the boredom is mental torture.

I am by nature a militant liberal except when it comes to child abuse or sex crimes.

I then transform myself into a Tory who is well to the right of Ian Duncan Smith.

My perfect punishment for child killers and rapists would be 30 years in solitary on a daily diet of stale bread and dirty water and then string them up.

The first 24 hours in Bellmarsh was a step into a dark and dangerous world.

As a teenager I'd lived in Children's homes, a Detention Centre, Redhill Special Unit and Borstal.

That was then and this is now.

My first impression was the constant noise. Non-stop shouting, the screaming and banging of doors.

I thought then and think now how will teenage murderers addicted to knife crime cope with being locked-up for Twenty years?

There`ll be no more girls, designer clothes and night clubs.

Will they still believe killing is cool?

The cowards will soon lose their swagger as they walk about in cheap tracksuits and go `night after night` without sex.

Their friends will be dancing, playing football, having fun, having kids and there`ll be rotting in a concrete coffin.

They will pay a heavy price for their cowardly crimes.

They`ll discover the days are long and extremely boring with lots of lows and few highs.

I woke up at 7am and spent five hours sitting on my bed and staring at the bare walls.

The flap on my cell door would open every 30 minutes and I`d see a creepy pair of eyes staring at me.

I was on suicide watch.

Bloody hilarious.

In the space of three days I`d gone from being a doting dad to a serial killer with a death wish.

I was according to the authorities mad, bad, dangerous and a suicide risk,

I wasn't any of the above but how soon would I get the chance to prove it?

My cell door was opened and three screws kitted out with truncheons, pepper sprays and walkie-talkies escorted me along a never-ending maze of corridors.

We went through a number of security doors and finally arrived in the Hospital Wing.

The three bulldog-headed thugs in military style black uniforms who all looked like pub landlord Al Murray handed me over to the medical staff.

I waited in the freezing corridor wondering what would happen next.

I was going to be sedated and force-fed drugs and transferred to a nice BUPA style room.

I wasn't even close.

A prison doctor summoned me into his consulting room and said:

"I doesn't look good Mr Johnson, unless you can satisfy us you're not mentally ill we can hold you here indefinitely".

Adding:

"You are looking at a life sentence".

I replied:

"I don't understand, you're joking.

There's been no trial and I've not been found guilty of anything".

He replied:

"There doesn't need to be a trial Mr Johnson, you've been sectioned under the Mental Health Act".

I was examined and asked a number of questions, the answers could determine the next 20 years of my life.

The interview /examination ended with a handshake and I returned me to my cell.

That evening a human being version of a screw opened my cell door and called me `Garry`.

I was asked if I wanted a radio or a television.

I chose TV so I could watch Match of The Day and see some pretty faces on the box.

I knew that a few glimpses of Amanda Holden or Kate Moss would lift my spirits and boost my morale.

I was expecting a large flat screen color TV but returned with the smallest black and white portable I'd ever seen.

It didn't have SKY Sports, but still felt like a gift from heaven.

I'm a born optimist. I thought I'd passed the test and maybe the Doctor had put in a good word for me.

I would find out the next day.

I won't bore you with details but once again did the long walk to the Hospital Wing.

I'm met by the black nurse with the Kojak haircut and Frank Bruno accent.

He became my confidante always advising me `to stop beating myself up about my daughter`.

The gentle giant escorted me to see the psychiatrist.

I had to prove I was not mentally ill by responding to a lot of probing questions and answering what I considered some silly ones.

It wasn't funny but fast becoming a joke.

How do you prove your sanity?

I was asked about the allegations which I assured him were false.

Once question stood out.

"How would you feel if I told you Richard Grimson had been by a bus and was dead".

Without hesitation I replied:

"I'd very happy".

He smiled saying:

"A perfectly normal reaction".

This examination went on for over an hour and I could sense it was going well.

It was obvious he doubted I was a mad.

The men in white coats seemed genuinely baffled by my case and like me couldn't understand what I was doing in a maximum security prison.

I had to wait a few more days for the official verdict on my sanity.

The Kojak lookalike handed me over to an officer who escorted me back to my cell.

There was a spring in my step and smile on my face. I was convinced I was going home.

But not yet.

I would spend another 48 hours in limbo watching rubbish programs on terrestrial TV which is only slightly better than staring at bare walls.

Solitary confinement scrambles your brain and plays tricks with your mind.

It dulls your senses so much you consider watching crap like The X Factor as entertainment.

I was given a big bag of sweets, a Mars bar, some fruit and a carton of milk, maybe I could get to like this.

I just needed an upgrade in my room service, a mini-bar and sexy blonde to share my bed.

The next day I was offered the chance of a shower and a clean change of clothes. But still no razor, comb or mirror.

I looked like a tramp but at least I smelt nice.

My conditions had improved and the screws were treating me like a human being but I was still in prison.

I was in isolation and away from the outside world.

I couldn't make any phone calls, write or receive letters and was denied any visitors.

The conditions seem even more harsh when you've not done anything wrong.

Prison life was nothing like the TV sit-com Porridge.

There were plenty of bolshie screws like Mr Mackay but no inmates resembling Norman Stanley Fletcher.

I`m taken to the Medical Wing where the black `Kojak` greets me with a handshake and words of wisdom.

He says:

"I`m read your files and you shouldn't be here".

I hoped the doctor agreed.

I wanted to hear it officially and on-the-record.

The truth, the whole truth and nothing but the truth on a legal document.

I was confident as I entered the room to hear my fate.

The doctor in the white coat was smiling so I guessed it was good news.

It was.

He said:

"You`ll be glad to know that the psychiatrist agrees with me Mr Johnson.

There is nothing wrong with you"

Adding:

"There are no signs of mental illness".

I replied:

"Thank you very much".

The case against me had fallen apart like a cheap suit.

At a later date three more psychiatrists would also give me a `clean bill of health`.

Dr Black, Dr Best and Forensic Psychiatrist Dr Sian Llewellyn-Jones.

She wrote:

"I am a consultant in Forensic Psychiatry at the John Howard Hospital in East London.

I have been asked by Essex Social Services to prepare a report on Garry Johnson.

I have been asked specifically whether or not he has any signs of mental illness.

Mr Johnson had a confident inter-personal style, a mood that was buoyant, almost to the point of elation, was talkative and he generally had an exuberant and `larger than life` quality.

Mr Johnson spoke was a middle-aged man who spoke with a marked Cockney accent and his manner was self-assured to the point of being expansive.

He was wearing a pale blue checked suit over a black shirt, these and his sunglasses, spikey hair and ready smile gave him a rather eccentric appearance.

Eccentricity is not a mental illness.

I would not describe Mr Johnson as having any mental health problems."

Dr Black agreed saying: "I am baffled as to why Essex Social Services consider Mr Johnson to be mentally ill.

I have met with this delightful gentleman on three separate occasions and detected no sign of mental illness."

I was no longer considered mad, bad or dangerous but couldn't just check out.

This was maximum security prison and not a hotel.

I was still a prisoner and not a guest.

There were forms to sign and paperwork to be completed it would be another three days before I was released.

My only visitor in 14 days of incarceration was a chatty Catholic Priest who like everyone else was shocked by my circumstances.

I must tell you a funny story.

I left a copy of Till Death Us Do Part in my cell and years later discovered it was passed around the prison.

Harry Harris became a bit of a bit hero. It`s why I brought him back in my novel Serial.

The morning of my release I was taken back to the see-through cage that I sat in on the night of my arrival.

This time it was crowded like the dancefloor of a gay night club.

There was no music but the noise was deafening.

A hundred blokes all talking at the same time. Blokes in expensive designer gear waiting to go to courts all over London.

The last time I`d seen so many men suited and booted was at a Wedding reception.

It was like a meeting of the United Nations.

The cage contained old men and teenagers of every colour, creed and nationality.

I noticed the various racial groups didn`t mix.

The only thing they had in common was the fact that they were all prisoners.

You could cut the atmosphere with a knife.

It`s only a matter of time before a violent race war erupts throughout the UK prison system.

My ex-wife and former father-in-law told people how they hoped I was having a hard time.

Julie even told a mutual friend: "I hope he dies in there and never comes out".

An opinion she repeated to our eldest child. Not on the phone or in a letter but on the streets of Wickford, shouting at my son:

"I hope your dad fucking dies".

The same message she`d scream at him across the street when she found out I was in a coma and on a life support machine.

She forgot about my `never say die` character and my personality.

I may not have been blessed with `good looks` but was born with the `gift of the gab`.

I had the God-given ability to get on with people.

I not only survived the hell of Bellmarsh but came out a better person.

The black Kojak with the Cockney accent was a clever bloke who got inside my head.

He advised me again and again:

"Stop beating yourself up about your daughter".

Adding:

"Make a success of your life then when she`s older she`ll be drawn towards you".

I took his advice on board and since my life-saving operation have followed it.

I`ve written songs, books and a film.

It would be six more years before the lies and false allegations of my ex-wife would put me back behind bars.

The drive from Bellmarsh in South East London to Basildon police station in Essex was bizarre and had no idea what awaited me.

Would the police would disagree with the medical and psychiatric experts.

I had no idea what was going to happen.

Would I be released, given bail or put on trial?

I wanted an apology for my false imprisonment.

I was handcuffed cuffed and freezing cold throughout the minute journey.

It was snowing heavily.

The prison van had no heating and I had no coat.

I`d left my Crombie, a Mars bar and my copy of Till Death Us Do Part in the cell.

I arrived at Basildon and was put in an underground cell below the Magistrates Court.

It was tiny with no windows and not much bigger than a public phone box.

I was suddenly released with no apology or explanation.

There were no TV cameras or tabloid journalists to witness my walk to freedom.

I walked straight into the arms of Diane, a very `special lady friend`.

She was joined by 2 members of my legal team.

Sue and Claire explained they`d been ordered by a Judge not to inform me about my imminent arrest.

They`d been gagged by the corrupt and fascist Family Court system.

These secret Hearings are essentially a `Kangaroo Court` infested with Nazi-style social workers, Gestapo Judges and in my case a lying ex-wife.

There is no Jury, no public gallery and the media are denied entry.

The corrupt proceedings all take place in secret and behind closed doors.

No evidence of `wrongdoing` is required as Judgements are based entirely on whatever lies the Mother has told to social workers.

I was unaware of any Hearings so did not attend or have the chance to defend myself.

I could not refute any of the false allegations made by my ex-wife.

Those who boast that "the British Justice system is the best in the world" have not been on the receiving end.

They have no idea what goes on behind closed doors or at an ex-parte Hearing.

I hugged both my solicitors and was told:

"We knew the allegations against you were rubbish and that you wasn't planning to kill us".

I shook my head and smiled as I didn't have a clue what they were talking about.

The police had only told me I was planning to kill my ex-wife and her boyfriend.

That was bollocks as was this latest revelation.

I was hearing more `fake news` than President Trump.

There was worse to come.

The Family Court had also been told I was planning to kill my children and then commit suicide.

My ex-wife had told a Gestapo-style secret court Hearing that I had a Hit List.

She had accused me of being a `serial killer` preparing to go on a murder spree.

My solicitors added:

"We wanted to tell you but were gagged by the Judge"

Adding:

"Had we told you Garry, we`d be in contempt of court and struck off".

It would be 72 hours before I`d hear the names on my so-called Hit List and given details of the `gagging order`.

It was like a story from Nazi Germany or Soviet Russia.

There was a funny side to all this.

I ended up in the legendary Private Eye magazine.

The Editor Ian Hislop is no fan of the British Courts and published my story.

He picked-up on the fact I`d written Till Death Us Do Part.

The write-up was hilarious.

I dare you to read it without laughing

The police confused me with Harry Harris but fellow journalists knew I wore three hats.

Depending on what I was wearing or the day of the week I was either showbiz writer Garry Johnson, author Garry Jackson or Punk Poet Gal Johnson.

The Private Eye exclusive exposed me as being all three at the same time to pull off a scam.

One of my tabloid colleagues had tipped off Fleet Street`s favorite magazine.

"Bloody hilarious" I thought.

I'm a great believer in the old saying:

'There is no such thing as bad publicity and I found it highly amusing'.

Ian Hislop or one of his team picked-up on a story I had published in The Sunday People and unlike the cops they could tell the difference between a fictional gangster and a tabloid journalist.

The police had thought I was Harry Harris but Private Eye knew my alias was Garry Jackson.

Confused?

Here is the story (word for word).

In a sensational Exclusive, the People revealed a few weeks ago at Robbie Williams is learning Cockney rhyming slang because he wants to play an East End gangster in a film.

"The pop superstar wants to ditch his Stoke-on-Trent accent to play an ex-boxer turned East London 'Mr Big'", it reported.

A source said, 'Robbie read about the character in a book called 'Till Death Us Do Part' and it blew him away.

But he knows he has got to sound like a Cockney if he wants the part."

The by-line on the story was GARRY JOHNSON, by an amazing coincidence, the author of 'Till Death Us Do Part' is Garry Jackson- a pseudonym of the self-same Garry Johnson.

His novel is published by New Breed Books, a firm run by a bulking bouncer named Jamie O'Keefe.

Unusually for a publishing house, it also offers classes in combat skills and self-defence.

Still the book comes with an ecstatic tribute from our old friend Garry Bushell, TV columnist for, er, the People:

"Bloody brilliant...if there's a better revenge novel around, I'd like to read it"

Johnson has been a mucker of the other Garry since the days of the Street Punk scene in the 1980s, when Bushell was lead singer of The Gonads and Johnson sang in The Buzz Kids.

Garry Johnson is also the author of 'The Story of Oi' and of a biography of Bushell, which can be found on the great man's website.

Alas, Inspector Knacker isn't as impressed as Bushell by 'Till Death Us Do Part', which seems to be based very loosely on Johnson's own marriage break-up, the main difference being that the protagonist enlists the help of the underworld to extract revenge on the unsavory character with whom his fictional wife has run off with.

Two weeks ago Johnson was arrested at his home in Wickford, Essex, and hauled off to Basildon police station, since Knacker had apparently interpreted the book as a `death threat`.

We trust this silly understanding will soon be cleared up, before Robbie Williams takes fright.

But he may still find Johnson`s publisher a bit scary.

In an interview four years ago with (inevitably) the People, Jamie O`Keefe declared, "If you road rage me while I have my children in the car, then I would not hesitate to come tearing through your front door at 5`o`clock in the morning and break every bone in your body before you wipe the sleep from your eyes.

I`ve done it a few times when it was deserved."

As Garry Bushell would say, "Bloody brilliant."

I re-print that write-up for a reason and not just because it`s a hilarious piece of writing by Private Eye.

It confirms when my ex-wife went to the police she was guilty of lying.

Julie knew exactly what she was doing.

She was making false allegations that would alarm the police and the Essex Criminal Mental Health Team.

The police and the CMHT should have read the book and discovered the truth before they decided to act on her tissue of lies.

It was two members of the Essex CMHT Sue Johnstone and Joe Delaney who contacted me within days of my release from prison.

They both came to my home to inform me they`d be taking no further action and expected me to be grateful.

I wasn't.

A verbal apology wasn`t enough I wanted a written apology which cleared my name.

They both agreed I was entitled and within a week I received a letter confirming `there was nothing wrong with me`.

It was personally delivered by Joe Delaney.

We got on so well he offered me a lift into town in his flashy red sports car.

Joe was a bit of a hippy and during the drive we talked about rock music, my sons and his daughter.

111

I never saw Sue Johnstone but stayed in touch with Joe Delaney as I knew he'd be a good contact.

He was.

The next time my ex-wife made more allegations about my mental health he spoke up on my behalf.

I was also visited by the police and to be honest it was more like a social call than a `them and us` situation.

It was if nothing had ever happened and there was no history between us.

I didn't want the police to be nice and friendly I wanted them to be professional.

If they'd done their job properly I would not have spent 2 weeks locked-up in a high security prison.

It was not rocket science.

They only had to read the book.

Harry Harris was not Garry Johnson. He was a fictional character.

He was an East End gangster and not a showbiz journalist.

He lived inside the pages of a novel at not at 22 Bridge Road Wickford.

He only had one victim and was not a serial killer.

`Till Death Us Do Part` was neither a death threat or even a secret.

The day before my arrest I was interviewed by the local paper and pictured holding a copy of the book.

It was no secret. I wasn't trying to hide it.

I was already an inmate in Bellmarsh when the article was published in the local paper.

They do say there is no such thing as "bad publicity" and it's true.

Till Death Us Do Part` by Garry Jackson got 50-plus rave reviews on Amazon.

The book is still listed so check them out.

It was only after my release that I understood why I'd been arrested and banged-up in Bellmarsh.

The authorities were given false information which they should have investigated and wrongly considered me a danger to society.

Basildon Police, Essex Social Services and the Essex Criminal Mental Health Team had been jointly conned by the vindictive lies of my ex-wife.

My legal team knew the truth and that I was more like Arthur Daley than Hannibal Lector.

I had my freedom but would take me five more years to clear my name completely.

It would include numerous court appearances at Basildon, Chelmsford, Southend, Romford, Colchester, Cambridge and The High Court in London.

I represented myself three times at the highest court in the land and eventually won.

Judge Moloney warned Essex Social Services: "Mr Johnson is a like a dog with a bone and will not go away".

Another added:

"He will fight with every fibre of his being".

I did.

Lord Justice Munby, the highest Judge in the land ruled I be given copies of transcripts.

Judge Moloney ordered Essex Social Services to handover all their documents.

I Fought the Law

Diane a lovely lady and `special friend` drove me home from the court. She was my rock.

The Paul Burrell to my Princess of Wales.

The 15-minute car ride was a journey of mixed emotions.

On one hand a dream-come-true situation on the other a step into the unknown.

As during those two weeks inside I genuinely didn't know when or if I would ever return home.

14 days doesn't sound long but as with life in the Big Brother house every day seems like a week.

I was told in prison that they could hold me indefinitely under the Mental Health Act and that the onus was on me to prove my sanity.

I want to take this opportunity to put on-the-record that Diane is one of the nicest people I`ve ever met.

She is also very pretty with a beautiful personality that equals her looks.

A stunner with a heart of gold, the sister I never had, the girlfriend I should have had.

I had not been this close to a woman for 2 weeks and to be honest there was movement in my boxer shorts.

If this was a movie we would have stopped off at the nearest hotel and spent all afternoon going at it like bunny rabbits.

This was reality and in real-life I`m a bit of a Gent and she is a proper Lady so nothing happened.

I am `old school` and in my world you don't mess with a married woman.

During the drive Diane told me about the whereabouts of Sam and Adam.

I`d been itching to know but scared to ask in case they`d been kidnapped by my ex-wife.

I was told she had tried but failed to snatch them.

It was now crystal clear why Julie had lied to the authorities and police.

She wanted me locked up so she could grab them.

That was her motive for lying, smearing my character and blackening my name.

The Hit List was a figment of her imagination to do me harm but her evil plan backfired.

Both boys refused to see her.

Adam moved in with Diane and Sam lived with Sara & Geoff, the parents of his best mate.

As we pulled up on the drive both my sons were waiting and rushed towards me.

We kissed, cuddled and laughed. We always laugh when we`re together as I am by nature a joker and would be comedian.

Or as my friends would say "a funny bastard".

I don't do `being down` or depression. My glass is always half full and never half empty.

I wanted to know how they`d been and what I`d missed.

That night we celebrated.

Sam and Adam.

Diane, her husband Paul and 3 children, Sara, Jeff and their 2 children all went into town for a Chinese meal.

It was nice to be home.

But this was just the calm before the storm.

What happened next moved things up a notch to a new and far more sinister level.

Essex police and Essex Social Services were getting tired of the endless allegations of Mrs Johnson so started to distant themselves from my ex-wife.

Julie was obviously not happy as she`d got used to the authorities jumping to her tune.

Advised by her solicitors she went back to court and took out Private Proceedings.

She applied in secret (ex-parte) for custody of the boys.

That failed so asked for the boys to be taken into care and become the property of the state.

She would rather they be locked-up than live with me.

The police acting on a Court Order surrounded our house back and front.

Both boys were dragged from their beds by 6 coppers and removed from the house by 3 escorts and a social worker.

Ten `brave` adults against a 12 and 10-year-old boy.

It was like a scene from Eastern Europe or South America.

Both boys struggled to get away but a burly cop warned them:

"I can use as much force as I want and believe me I will"

If anyone doubts a word of this I am more than happy to take a Lie Detector Test.

The front garden of my house was full of coppers, nosey neighbours and various onlookers including social worker Peter Brown.

None of them knew what I knew.

This time I`d been given advanced warning that something like this might happen.

We were prepared.

The boys had money and a mobile phone hidden in their trousers.

They were not searched before being bundled into a van with three escorts.

I was calm and collected which puzzled the police and Peter Brown because I knew it was only the beginning and not the end.

The next few years would be like an X-rated soap opera involving politicians, national newspapers, gangsters, safe houses including a hide-out 100 yards from the EastEnders studio.

An hour later I got a phone call from Sam:

"Dad, were on the platform at Grays railway station."

So, what had happened?

They`d been driven to a Social Services hostel in Chafford Hundred Grays and as soon as the escort`s van drove off they runaway.

I told them to sit tight and that I was on my way.

An hour later we`re re-united and both boys spend the night in a safe house.

They are safe from the clutches of Peter Brown and Essex Social Services.

It was easy to hide them as I had plenty of volunteer helpers and many options.

The school Summer holidays had just started so there was no pressure and I had seven weeks to play with.

At various times they were given shelter by my dad and the women I mentioned earlier.

Justine, Diane, Kelly, Jodie, Karen and Samantha.

They also stayed at safe houses in South London, Canvey Island, and Southend-on-Sea.

A flat in Laindon and stayed at a hide-out in Elstree belonging to the ex-wife of a mate from football.

The lady was a former police officer who took a statement from both boys in which they revealed their terrible treatment by Social Services.

I was ordered back to court so many times during this 8-year period I was on first name terms with the security guys.

The police came to the house more times than my postman.

I'd leave the key in the front door so they could come in and search without waking me up.

At first the police treated us like serious criminals, coming mob handed and carrying out early morning raids.

One night the boys were captured and taken to a Social Services hostel in Southend-on-Sea.

This was no `big deal` as we'd already discussed the escape plan.

The next morning as agreed they absconded and went straight to McDonalds for breakfast.

They phoned with details of the great escape.

A `friend of a friend` contacted a top solicitor.

The guy was Alan Foskett.

A legal eagle who went out of his way to help Sam and Adam.

A lovely bloke who went that extra mile and reminded me of Arthur Daley.

Arthur is my all-time TV hero so I can pay him no higher compliment.

Alan Foskett was my favourite type of person.

A East End boy made good who still had his Cockney accent.

Alan Foskett was fearless and a member of the Children`s Panel.

He was not a run-of-the-mill Legal Aid solicitor but an expert in his field.

Social Services would dare not mess with a bloke like this.

The funniest moment was when Judge Roderick Newton accused Mr Foskett of helping Sam and Adam to escape from custody.

Alan was not amused but never charged with any offence. The boys loved him.

Mr Foskett described my case as "the worst he had ever came across".

Adding:

"For the first time in my career I feel ashamed of my profession".

Alan Foskett like Lord Justice Munby and Judge Moloney was one of the good guys.

He was not shy to go public and embraced the media.

Jumping ahead.

Mr Foskett told The Daily Mail:

"Sam and Adam are not subject to any gagging order".

He also discussed the case with MPs John Baron and John Hemming.

My eldest son gave an interview to The Daily Mail and the case was discussed on SKY News, Good Morning Britain, The Times and The Sun.

I twice appeared on Talk Radio using an alias and appeared on a This Morning phone-in.

Camilla Cavendish of The Times, now Dame Camilla Cavendish met me when I attended The High Court and wrote a very moving article in her newspaper column.

Alan Foskett was involved so Essex Social Services had to stop bending the rules and treating me like a criminal.

A few days later Sam and Adam returned home and went back to school.

Mrs Johnson was furious and again tried to get the boys removed.

Social Services didn't want to get involved but because of her Proceedings the Judge ordered them to take action.

This was ironically an order by Judge Roderick Newton.

Have we heard that name before?

It`s the same Judge Roderick Newton who in December 2013 would revoke the `Gagging Orders` and give permission for me to tell my story.

A week is a long time in politics and 8 years is a long time in a custody battle.

I had the last laugh, but didn't get to celebrate at the time as I was in a coma and on a life support machine.

I bet he never imagined when granting my ex-wife permission for her Private Proceedings that years later he would be forced into a U-Turn.

I wish Julie and I had both been present to witness him revoke his draconian Orders.

I would have smiled and loved to have seen the look on her face.

The Judge ruled I could write about anything and everything including 'Saturday Night Specials' and my war with Essex Social Services.

I doubt Julie would have joined me in a celebration glass of champagne.

Let us go back in time.

My ex-wife had a partial win with her Private Proceedings victory but in name only as Sam and Adam were now teenagers and not young boys.

Like me they were born rebels.

It was part of their DNA.

They believed like me that bad rules are there to be broken.

Social Services turned up they run away.

The police brought them back.

They run away. It was like a game of hide and seek.

The police chased them all over Wickford.

Adam got away but Sam was caught.

This time they locked him in a cell but within hours he'd be free again.

Alan Foskett intervened and Sam was released.

My ex-wife was not happy and again she contacted Peter Brown.

My guess is she had him on speed dial.

Brown turned up on our doorstep and for the first time Sam told him to "Fuck off."

The little boy was now a 6ft teenager who would no longer allow himself to be intimidated by a middle-class social worker.

He'd had enough.

Peter Brown being the 'brave soldier' that he was did exactly what he'd been told

He couldn't get away quick enough.

I`m not sure what happened next but either Brown or Mrs Johnson contacted the police.

I got another visit and was asked "are Sam and Adam still living with you?"

They knew the answer so why bother to lie?

I said "Yes they are".

Instead of asking to come in or wanting to speak with both boys the coppers turned on their heels and walked away.

The next day Sam was spotted over the park and they put him in the back of a police car but this time they`d come in peace.

The war was over.

It ended like that famous scene when Neville Chamberlin returned from his meeting with Adolf Hitler waiving a piece of paper.

This time it was an official Essex Police document signed by a Sergeant.

They no longer wanted to be involved.

Sam was told "We`ve got better things to do with our time than chase you and your brother all over the place. From now on Social Services can do their own dirty work".

Adding:

"if you can talk your brother into giving himself up and coming to meet we`ll leave you alone."

Adding:

"We`ll then take you wherever it is you want to go".

Sam said:

"To our dad`s house."

The copper said:

"We can`t do that, but we`ll take you anywhere else of your choice".

He added:

"But wherever you go after that is up to you."

Sam contacted his brother and both boys spent the night at Justine`s.

The same Justine Salmon that Social Services and the Family Court had warned to have no contact with the boys.

She was/is a lovely lady who went beyond the call of duty to help both Sam and Adam.

I have so many women to thank for all their help since Julie left.

It`s not just me whose made their beds, cooked meals, washed and ironed clothes.

I must pay tribute to every single one of my female army of volunteers.

Justine, Diane, Sarah, Jodie, Kelly, Samantha, Karen.

The Magnificent Seven who cared for my boys and helped me to win the war.

The next day the police turn up at Justine`s with a updated copy of the official letter.

It confirmed the police wanted no more involvement with Sam and Adam.

Justine was told a copy of the letter would also be sent to Social Services.

I thought back to when Peter Brown boasted: "We never lose".

He just had.

The game was over.

Social Services and The Family Courts were powerless to do anything without the police.

They were there `boots on the ground`.

Peter Brown was like a defeated General with no troops.

My ex-wife was spitting feathers and running around like a headless chicken.

They do say a wounded animal is at its most dangerous when cornered.

The same can be said of a desperate woman running out of options.

My ex-wife had lost the support of the police and without them Social Services were as much use as a toothless tiger.

Julie teamed-up with a new friend. A woman who was more than one sandwich short of a picnic.

I won`t name her because she would love the notoriety.

She is one of only Five people I won`t name in this book for very different reasons.

Two because they are `famous/infamous` and were on my side and really helped me out.

They did things to help me which I know the authorities would not appreciate.

You would have to kill me to get their names and even than I`d give you false ones.

Number three I'll call `The Third person`.

This is because I don't know him, never met him and not sure if he even knows his name was put in the frame.

The other two unmentionables are both females who were part of `Team Julie`.

I'll always refer to the fame hungry Glory Hunters as `Ginger` and `Geezer Bird`.

They would both love nothing more than the prestige of being named in a book.

It would be the highlight of their pathetic lives so I won't name them.

Sorry guys, you're not getting any free publicity in my book. Write your own.

They both have a soap opera connection and are dead-ringers for fictional barmaids,

`Ginger` is the spitting image of Corrie barmaid Liz McDonald and `Geezer Bird` could be the twin of Eastenders pint-puller Shirley Carter.

`Ginger` was abusive to my mum and told her she couldn't see Lucy.

`Geezer Bird` told my sons unless they spoke to Julie they'd be shot boasting:

"It would take one phone call to (the man I call the 3rd person) and he'd shoot you".

I had never heard of the bloke but contacts had.

He was a criminal but not the sort who'd harm children.

This bloke was `old school` who certainly wouldn't shoot schoolboys.

The next time `Geezer Bird` went further claiming "He'll shoot you and your dad.

It will only take one phone call".

She saw me in the street and started bragging:

"My friend was the hardest bloke in British prisons".

This was a lie as his surname was not Bronson or Sykes.

She added:

"He controls the London Underworld".

Another lie as his surname was not Adams, Hunt or Arif.

She went on:

"Last week he went around to the house of footballer Joey Cole (West Ham & England) threatened to break his legs and took £25,000 grand off him".

Adding:

"Yesterday he turned over Dagenham Football Club, threatened the Manager with a shotgun and took £50,000 off him".

I`m not sure but suspected she was bi-polar.

She spoke like a speed-freak and fired anecdotes like machine gun bullets.

Spraying boasts like confetti with each one getting less and less believable.

She added:

"And he threatened TV star Bradley Walsh said he`d shoot him if he didn`t handover £50,000".

I knew that was bollocks as Bradley is a close friend of a good mate of mine.

He`s also related to the biggest crime family in London.

Even the American Mafia wouldn`t be brave enough to mess with the TV funnyman.

She added:

"And if I ask him he`ll shoot you for nothing. It will only take one phone call".

I said sarcastically:

"Thanks for letting me know much appreciated but the boys still ain`t talking to Julie".

I thought to myself not only is this woman deranged, she`s also pretty stupid.

She`s saying all this to a journalist.

I wondered if `the third person` would be happy about this woman putting his name in the frame?

I had no idea if the Joey Cole or the Dagenham Football Club story were true, but if they were I`m sure he`d really appreciate her telling everyone.

Whatever the truth of her bragging, fact or fiction, it was no concern of mine though the threats to my children were.

I didn't take them seriously to start with and even less after I checked `Geezer Bird` out.

The women was a complete fantasist who thought she was a female gangster.

A `Billy no mates` who watched Eastenders and idolised Queen Vic landlady Shirley Carter.

They had the same haircut and facial features but one was a good actress the other was a fantasist.

Four more big boasts convinced me she was a compulsive liar and a 5t^h was an own goal which did Julie no favours.

1. She was once engaged to Arsenal & England footballer Ray Parlour.

She wasn't.

2. Alan Brazil the former Ipswich & Scotland footballer Alan Brazil was a great friend who loaned her his private box at the 02 Stadium.

He wasn't.

3. She was friends with football pundit and radio host Mike Parry.

She wasn't.

The great thing about being a journalist is that you're expert in checking things out.

You can always contact people direct or through senior colleagues.

A tabloid journalists phone book is like a Yellow Pages of celebrity.

Ray Parlour, Alan Brazil and Mike Parry were all contacted and would you believe not one of them had ever heard of this woman.

Boast number 4 also turned out to be another figment of her imagination.

Geezer Bird told my sons and their friends that one night she was in a pub with the `3rd man` when he phoned one of the top men in the UK underworld.

She claimed her friend warned him to "stay away" from a high-profile funeral.

I knew this was a lie. I knew the person concerned plus I use the Internet.

I showed Sam and his friends some clips on You Tube.

The guy I know not only attended the funeral but gave a reading.

It was lie number 5 that helped me to win my case. It was a whopper and played a major role in my victory against Social Services.

The fantasist friend of my ex-wife told me:

"I'm good friends with the MP John Baron and I can get him to have a word with Social Services about you.

I'll get him to help Julie".

It was a big mistake to say something like that to a journalist.

My immediate thought was of scandal, corruption and collusion in high places.

If this was true and a politician was involved in covering-up child abuse the press would be all over it.

Was a top politician really involved?

I contacted John Baron and introduced myself as journalist Garry Johnson.

He was genuinely shocked by the allegations and assured me had never heard of this woman.

John Baron was a lovely bloke and we got on like a house on fire.

He was an ex-Army officer and as honest as they come

I guess because I was a journo he insisted in putting his denial in writing and on-the record.

With or without Julie's knowledge her friend had scored a massive own goal on her behalf.

John Baron MP was one of 'the good guys' and without the interference of Julie's fantasist friend we would never have met.

He would become one of my major allies in my war against social services.

It was John who invited me to Parliament and got my name mentioned on the floor of the House of Commons.

He also spoke to the media on my behalf.

The last word on Julie's friend as well as being a fantasist she was also a police grass.

I don't mean making anonymous calls to Crime-stoppers I'm talking about an official registered grass and I have the documents to prove it.

Printed in bold black letters on white paper is her name and address.

Julie's friend is no real-life 'Shirley Carter' but she is a genuine Bertie Smalls.

A Wickford version of the infamous London bank robber who turned super-grass.

I ignored the Court Orders, the boys ignored Peter Brown and my ex-wife was spitting feathers.

She went ballistic as for the first time in years both the police and Peter Brown were not dancing to her tune.

The boys were officially staying with Justine who only lived a ten minute walk from mine so were back home whenever they wanted.

Mrs Johnson was out of control. She hit Sam in the street and drove her car at Adam.

Julie didn't try and kill him.

She pulled up onto the pavement and pinned him against a wall.

This was outside his school and in front of so many onlookers.

She blocked him in and was shouting and screaming like a women possessed.

Two ladies came banging on my door d I reported it to my solicitor.

Social Services were not interested.

The harassment was non-stop.

Julie chased Adam out of a local supermarket, up and down Wickford High Street and all round Shotgate Park.

Adam fled and was almost struck by a car.

She confronted Sam in the street and tried to grab him outside Justine`s house.

Peter Brown would still visit but social services refused to take any form of action.

His new role was that of Mrs Johnson`s messenger boy.

Pete the postman turned up with an offer that he thought we couldn't refuse.

He said:

"If the boys agree to see her, then Mrs Johnson will let them see their sister".

I was not included.

Sam and Adam declined the offer unless I got to see my daughter.

Peter Brown had a new opinion to go with his `new job` as Julie`s messenger boy.

A sudden change of heart.

He was now in favour of Lucy seeing me and claimed to be "working on Mrs Johnson".

I know what you`re thinking if the police are no longer involved why am I still talking to Peter Brown?

The answer is simple.

Family Courts are a law to themselves and Social Services threatened to involve them.

I was told unless you co-operate we`ll support Mrs Johnson when she starts Private Proceedings.

Peter Brown softened the pill by making me an offer I couldn`t refuse.

If I would agree to it he promised to get Mrs Johnson off both our backs.

What was the offer?

It was something I had not heard of. It was obvious Social Services wanted out.

If I agreed to sign a document called a `Living At Home With Parent` agreement` it would mean both boys could live with me legally.

What was the catch? What was the benefit in signing?

There would be no more court cases and they would no longer co-operate with any Private Proceedings.

Peter Brown said:

"This is a big gesture on our part. These documents are seldom used and we don`t offer them lightly".

Adding:

"If you sign you`ll only see me for about 10 minutes maybe once or twice a month".

I signed.

This might have got Julie Johnson off Brown`s back but once again I was in the firing line.

My ex-wife was about to make fresh allegations that would further alienate Sam and Adam.

False Allegations

I was arrested and once again handcuffed in front of Sam and Adam.

The boys already disliked her but these latest allegations made them hate her.

This time she had concocted a malicious masterplan with her child-abusing lover and best friend `Ginger`.

Together they conspired to set me up with another false allegation involving `revenge porn`.

It conned the authorities and briefly led to me being banged-up in a cell.

It also triggered a life-long negative reaction from Sam and Adam.

They already dis-liked her for condoning the vile behavior of her perverted boyfriend.

They now hated her even more.

They were not impressed with her lying to the police and getting their Dad locked-up once again.

My sons were involved in the arrest.

The house was surrounded by a dozen cops who turned up in two squad cars and a van.

This fact can be confirmed by both my sons who were at home and harshly dealt with by the police.

Sam was dragged off his laptop and Adam followed to the bathroom.

A copper even stood guard as an innocent child went to the loo.

It was like a scene from a movie as both boys shouted and swore at the cops.

I was handcuffed, dragged out of the house and assaulted.

My sons were both shouting "It`s her again, this is down to her Dad".

They were not wrong. Only this time the coppers didn't just target me they searched my son`s bedrooms and removed both their laptops.

On arrival at Basildon Police Station I was put in a cell and told "You`re in serious trouble".

I knew I was innocent but what good had that done me previously.

The so-called British justice system does not apply to working class people like me.

In the eyes of the law `you are guilty until you prove your innocence`.

I paced up and down trying to guess what on earth I`d been accused of this time.

I soon found out.

My ex-wife had told the police I`d posted clips of her porn movies and naked pictures on the internet.

As with all previous allegations she had provided no hard evidence.

The police had no screen grabs or video clips.

I was taken to an Interview Room and told "Mr Johnson we believe you have posted pornographic material on the Internet"

Adding:

"You should be aware we`ve searched your property and removed your computer, both your laptops and those of your children".

This meant both boys had to go 2 months without playing Football Manager.

I was asked:

"Do you deny it?"

I replied:

"Yes, 100 per cent."

One of the cops opened a folder and placed various pornographic photographs on the desk asking:

"Do you recognise the woman in the pictures?"

I laughed, not because I thought it was funny, but because of the stupidity of his question.

I replied:

"Well of course I know her, I was married to her for 15 years, but those pictures have nothing to do with me"

Copper:

"So, who is the lady in the pictures?"

Me:

"My ex-wife"

Copper:

"So, you admit the lady in the pictures is Julie Johnson?"

Me:

"Obviously, I can`t deny that, but the pictures have nothing to with me".

Yes, the naked Polaroid pictures were of my ex-wife but I wasn't the photographer.

Julie was so desperate to fit me up she`d posed for new pictures in the hope of getting me into trouble.

She`d do anything if it meant getting me locked-up and losing custody of the boys.

Julie was `happy` for complete strangers to see her wearing nothing but a smile and a pair of black stockings if it could damage.

The two cops were wearing uniforms but at the end of the day they were still men.

What must they have thought when she made the allegation and saw the pictures?

How about a date?

They obviously appreciated a pretty face and a nice body because they believed her story.

They kept calling me a `liar` and pressuring me to confess.

I said:

"If you study the pictures, not her body, her face and look at the length of her hair.

You`ll see those pictures are all pretty recent.

She has got straight shortish hair in every one of them.

That`s what Julie looks like now so they can`t have anything to do with me.

I haven`t taken any porn pictures of her since about 1995/1996.

The last time she posed for me my ex-wife had really long blonde hair.

I can tell you those pictures were not taken at 64 Chestnut Road".

Adding:

"Why would we have wasted our time with a Polaroid camera when we we`re making films?"

My final thought got them thinking:

"I have not been alone with Julie since 2005. I only see her in court so where or how would I get the opportunity to take porno pictures of her?

Why don't you go back and check her hairstyle?

130

It`s exactly the same now as it is in those pictures".

Adding:

"Sorry but you`re talking to the wrong bloke".

After an hour of relentless questioning I`m returned to my cell and released the next morning.

I`m on unconditional bail and told to report back in 8 weeks.

The police IT experts kept my computer, 2 laptops and children`s laptops for two months.

All charges were dropped.

They found nothing because there was nothing to find.

I was 100 per cent innocent of all charges and don't just take my word for it.

Let me quote `word for word` from the letter from my criminal lawyers Nelson Guest & Partners sent to my Family Law solicitors HKH & Cox Solicitors:

"We understand that you act on behalf of Garry Johnson in connection with a matter of Family Law.

We are asked to write in respect of a contact application made by our mutual client in respect of his daughter Lucy, who he has not seen for some considerable time.

We understand the basis of this are allegations made by his ex-wife about various matters relating to Mr Johnson and things that he is supposed to have done.

We can tell you that our involvement in this matter is to act on his behalf when he was arrested in relation to allegations made by his ex-wife, that had posted on the internet.

We can tell you that following a police investigation this was found not to be the case and that all the allegations were for want of a better way of putting it malicious on the part of her.

He has not been subject to any prosecution and it is quite clear that the matter was for want of a better expression manipulated by her to reflect upon him.

But that he had not done anything which could or should be regarded as wrong doing."

And the Police agreed.

All charges were dropped, my computers and lap tops returned.

Essex police found no evidence because there was none to find.

My solicitors were not happy with the conduct of the police and advised I made a complaint.

A `clear the air` meeting was arranged with Inspector Sage.

The Inspector was the Head of Wickford Police.

We met and I found him to be a very nice guy.

He had what I call `people skills` and apologised for the bully boy behaviour his surly Sergeant.

A man he described as "a bit of a hothead who'd recently arrived from the Metropolitan Police".

Inspector Sage made the following promise:

"If your ex-wife makes more allegations I promise we won`t just turn up on your doorstep mob handed.

We will ring first and ask when would be a convenient time to call".

Sorted.

I heard no more from police again but it wasn't the end of the harassment.

Once more my ex-wife recruited Essex Social Services to try and destroy me.

Social workers are the closest thing to the Gestapo and more corrupt then a Russian politician.

They threw down the gauntlet and as is my character I picked it up.

Essex social worker Peter Brown was a dead-ringer for The Simpsons character Principal Skinner.

He told me: "we never lose so don't waste your time fighting us".

I did fight and eventually I won.

It was not easy but once Essex Social Services were ordered by the courts to handover all their secret documents the truth came flooding out.

They were powerless to stop it.

I won custody of my sons and a verbal apology from Nicky O`Shaugnessy.

This was followed by a written apology from her successor and new Head of Essex Social Services Helen Lincoln.

The last I heard social worker Peter Brown was on `extended gardening leave`.

There was a funny moment in court when Judge Moloney revealed: "Peter Brown is not a well man, it seems the case has taken a heavy toll on his health".

I smiled and Sam cheered as if we were at a West Ham football match.

The Judge gently rebuked my son saying "Please tell Sam to calm down Mr Johnson".

It was a great day when Judge Moloney ordered Essex Social Services to handover their files but five years of fighting the system had taken a massive toll on my health.

Outside court I collapsed with the first of my 5 heart attacks.

Judge Moloney approached Sam as I was being stretchered off into the ambulance saying

"Tell your Dad I wish him well".

Four more heart attacks, 2 triple heart by-pass operations and numerous court appearances would follow as I fought to be reunited with my daughter.

This is my story.

Working Class Hero

I was born in a house in Hackney with an outside loo and have never forgotten my working class roots.

I grew up listening to my grandad talking about the Second World War and Battle of Cable Street.

He was proud of the time patriotic EastEnders defeated Hitler and stood shoulder to shoulder with Jewish neighbours to defeat Sir Oswald Mosley and his Blackshirts.

Between leaving school and joining the work force I was, and at the same time wasn't just like every other teenager.

At 15 I was into all the usual things like football, girls, music, cinema and alcohol.

I would soon become a David Bowie fanatic addicted to all things sex, drugs and rock & roll.

Before Ziggy Stardust life was all about playing football and I had trials with West Ham, QPR. Leyton Orient and Southend United.

I called myself the "white Pele" or the "Cockney Georgie Best". My ambition was to be a professional footballer.

I soon grew out of that.

A year after leaving school I was only interested in blue-eyed blondes, fast drugs and going to gigs.

I quickly discovered I wasn't cut-out for a 9 to 5 job.

I couldn't conform to a suburban lifestyle so left home to seek fame & fortune.

At 18 I was hanging-out in the West End of London and sleeping `wherever I could lay my hat`.

My `teenage wildlife` would last another 10 years and although it was great fun couldn't last forever.

I'd taken vast amounts of `fast drugs`, slept with many women, made and lost a lot of money.

But something was missing.

I wanted to be a dad.

I needed to meet a female of the species who ticked all the right boxes.

Not just a pretty face with long legs and blonde hair. I wanted a soul mate.

A best friend I could have kids with and ideally looked like Suzanne Mitzi.

We met Julie at an East End Wedding.

I was a friend of the groom. She was a friend of the bride.

It was perfect timing as in a way we were both single and on the market.

Julie had just ended her affair with a married man and the children`s nanny I`d been seeing returned home to South Africa.

The minute she walked into the room I knew I`d found what I`d been looking for.

She was drop-dead gorgeous, owned a car and laughed at all of my jokes.

It was mutual appreciation.

She stole my heart and I swept her off her feet.

Our first few months together were the happiest time of my life.

Being in love was better than drugs, all-night parties, sleeping around and getting drunk.

Much more fun than all those things put together.

She was just 21 and eight years younger than me.

A classic beauty admired by the masses whereas I am an acquired taste who could never be described as a hunk.

Even at my peak I wasn't handsome.

I`d never relied on my looks and always used my eccentric personality and `gift of the gab` to attract women.

But the truth is Julie fancied me almost as much as I fancied her.

I was one lucky bastard and I knew it.

From day one I wanted us to live together and Christmas came early when she agreed to move in.

We cut ourselves off from the outside world and spent weekends snuggled up in bed or on the sofa.

We were like a couple of hermits rarely leaving the privacy of the flat.

We were a drug-free zone with sexual highs replacing the need for speed, cocaine or alcohol.

We did nothing but make love, laugh and talk.

It wasn't sex it was making love.

We were truly, deeply, madly in love and just wanted each other.

There was no night-clubbing, pubs or visitors to the flat.

Like Greta Garbo we both just wanted to be alone.

They do say `opposites attract` and in our case it was true.

Julie hated drugs, wasn't a drinker and thought David Bowie was a "poof".

Her words not mine.

It had to be love as I allowed her to insult my life-long hero.

She was also the only person allowed to smoke weed or Marlboro cigarettes in my flat.

As a fanatical non-smoker, that was a massive gesture on my part.

We spent every night of the week at the flat and at weekends never bothered getting dressed.

It was all about sex, pushing the boundaries and making memories.

Within a month I knew she was the one for me.

The pretty face, the blonde hair, the long legs, the pert bum and as her clothes labels confirmed, the perfect 10.

We were married within Three months and a year later I was a dad.

It was without doubt the proudest moment of my life. We had a son called Sam and life could not be any better.

So you ask, what went wrong?

I can answer that.

For me the gloss was taken off our perfect relationship by her family.

The truth is I loved Julie too bits and not embarrassed to admit my true feelings.

I will not lie even if it risks being ridiculed and labelled as a wimp.

The fact is I genuinely adored her.

I had for fallen in love for the first time in my life but unfortunately she wasn't an orphan.

Julie had parents.

She came with excess baggage.

They were called parents and if I wanted her I had to accept her extended family.

I was tempted to make my excuses and leave but I`d fallen head over heels.

They future in-laws were everything she was not.

Ugly on the inside and out, small minded, old fashioned and bigoted.

I did not want any part of this but they came as a package. If you like a `job lot`.

I wanted a wife and kids but no way did I want the in-laws from hell.

I didn`t sign up for that and hoped that once we were married we could move away.

We did, but they followed like a bad smell and moved to a house about 300 yards from our front door.

I did not like them and they never liked me. We were like chalk and cheese.

They were right-wing Conservatives bordering on National Front.

I was a working-class liberal.

They were old-fashioned, small-minded and behaved like OAPs even though they were in their Fifties.

My former father-in-law was one of those men who always expected his dinner on the table.

He was an armchair general who shouted at the TV whenever a black person read the news.

Only once did I have the misfortune to go on a day out with them.

Sam and Adam were about Six and Four and we all went to Southend-on-Sea for the day.

It was a nightmare.

At 3pm on the dot the Taylors wanted lunch. We walked up and down the High Street in search of what they called "suitable food".

They wouldn't eat Indian or Chinese.

Turning their noses up at McDonalds, Burger King, Pizza Hut and Wimpy.

Mr Taylor saying: "We won`t eat foreign muck or fast food".

I walked off with Julie and we took both boys for a Happy Meal.

When we met up later the in-laws from hell were both happy as they`d found a `proper` English café which served a traditional Sunday Roast.

That was the first and final time I ventured out into public with Julie`s pathetic parents.

They were like a couple of old social dinosaurs stuck in another era.

I couldn`t cope with their old-fashioned ways and bigoted opinions.

It was mutual loathing and the only thing we had in common was Julie.

I am by nature a friendly sort of bloke who gets on with most people and talks to anyone.

So, at first, I thought `Oh it`ll be alright` as I`ll probably only have to see them 2 or 3 times a year and maybe every other Christmas.

I was wrong. Very wrong. My bloody in-laws weren`t just for long-distance phone calls and flying visits.

Like a puppy dog at Christmas they were for life (or in my case until I got divorced).

A few months after Julie moved into my flat they bought a house in the next street.

The `out-laws` were now living 300 yards from my front door

We were married for Fifteen years and during that period I never stopped loving her or started liking her parents.

I`m proud to say that not once did I go to the pub with my father-in-law.

It`s true what they say, you can choose your friends, but not your extended family.

I was high on coke the night we met at that wedding and the day she moved in.

I mention this because Julie knew and approved of my rock & roll lifestyle.

She always knew I preferred `fast drugs` to alcohol. It was a massive part of my social life.

As it is was then and is today with everyone from celebs to middle-class professionals.

I was never addicted. It never controlled me as I was always in control.

I just loved the euphoria and enjoyed the feeling of always being `up`.

The buzz it gave suited my fun-loving character.

At first Julie thought it was funny that I hardly slept, rarely ate and never stopped talking.

I made her laugh with my jokes and routines.

Every night I`d have a few lines of coke or speed beside the bed with a bottle of vodka.

That along with a slice of marmite on toast would be my breakfast.
It would set me up for the day and had been my routine for years.
But when Julie said she wanted a baby I stopped.
I replaced `fast drugs` with black coffee, caffeine drinks and Guarana Juice from the Holland & Barratt health shop.
It tasted vile but gave me a slight high.
I was a teetotal, drug-free vegetarian and 6 months later I became a dad.
The day my son Sam was born was the proudest moment of my life.
I took to being a dad like a duck to water and, as is my character, I wanted more.
You`ve heard me say that before, but it`s true. If I like something or someone I have to have more.
I am an addict who always becomes obsessed and hooked on things that make me happy and feel good.
David Bowie, fast drugs, marmite, Julie, Sam, Adam, Lucy, family life.
I will never say a bad word about any of them.
Sam was two when Adam was born and for the first time in my life I was truly and genuinely happy.
Fatherhood was better than sex, drugs, and Rock & Roll put together.
Who needed white lines when you could get hugs and kisses from your children?
I was far happier changing smelly nappies then I was snorting lines of cocaine.
I know what you`re thinking, "two isn`t enough"
And you`d be correct in making that assumption.
I loved being a dad so much I wanted more.
But it weren`t that easy.
Sam and Adam sort of came-on-demand. No problems, no delays.
Julie wanted to get pregnant and she did.
But scoring a hat-trick wasn't so easy.
Lucy had to be one of the most wanted and tried for babies in the world.
It took three years to get lucky.
At first it was no hardship as we were going at it like rabbits, doing it every day.

It was great fun, but as the months dragged on it became a worry.

There was no 'Bullseye' moment, we were not 'hitting the target' so to speak.

To be honest, Julie was wearing me out. I was losing weight and she was losing patience.

Like me, she was desperate for a daughter to complete our perfect family.

She stopped smoking, changed her diet and raided her 'dressing up box' on a nightly basis.

It wasn't always as much fun as it sounds.

I'd be so tired even with Julie dressed as a sexy French Maid or St Trinians schoolgirl it'd be more of a chore than pleasure.

When role playing didn't work she decided on another plan of action.

After sex she'd put her back against the wall and raise her legs towards the ceiling.

My job was to hold her ankles and encourage my sperm to find her eggs.

Julie was so desperate to get pregnant she soon decided I was the 'problem'.

She changed my diet, stopped me drinking tea and coffee or wearing tight pants.

I was force fed Zinc tablets and made to have cold baths before coming to bed.

When this didn't work either she rubbed ice cubes on my bollocks and ice poles on my penis.

Sex was becoming a chore so no wonder we made porn films.

They saved our marriage.

You need some excitement when sex in the bedroom is reduced to a clinical plan of action.

Where every time I'd 'cum', I had to jump up, grab her ankles and hold her legs in the air.

It was a great view, but after a while even the Taj Mahal can look ordinary.

This didn't work, so Julie came up with yet another solution which came from a woman's magazine rather than a medical expert.

Don't laugh, but she read rubbing Lettuce leaves into our private parts guaranteed a daughter.

I'm telling you this confidential information and revealing all about my embarrassing visits to Basildon Hospital to show how much Lucy was wanted by us both.

Julie was examined first and as she predicted passed every test with flying colours.

There was nothing wrong with her internal works and plumbing.

Was the problem me?

Well, according to Julie it had to be and Basildon Hospital agreed.

Tests confirmed the punk poet was firing blanks and had a low sperm count.

I was given tablets, a diet sheet and Julie relished taking control of the situation.

I found myself living on a strict diet of tuna fish, salmon, prawns and fish fingers.

I was drinking pints of cranberry juice and taking so many Zinc tablets I rattled when I walked.

My only act of defiance was refusing to privately masturbate into the sample jar.

I had not wanked since Julie moved in, as we had an agreement.

If I really wanted to 'cum my whack' as Julie put it, and she wasn't in the mood for intercourse.

And those rare occasions happen.

I'd cum between her tits, the cheeks of her bum or in her mouth.

The longer we were together the more she enjoyed the pleasure of oral sex.

The only proviso being my penis had to be fresh, clean and almost glowing in the dark.

During our marriage my dick would sparkle more than the crown jewels.

As I always wanted a blow job anytime, anywhere, anyplace, I must have had the cleanest knob in the UK.

There was nothing sexist in my addiction to oral sex as Julie shared my fondness.

Julie loved me going down on her at every opportunity.

Sometimes she'd be so out of control she'd leak more than a burst pipe.

As a precaution we'd spread out a bath towel on top of the bed.

So Julie would get me going and then I'd pull away and ejaculate into the sample jar.

We'd get dressed in a hurry and rush it straight to Basildon hospital.

As you can imagine it wasn't much fun walking into the specimen department and handing it over to some woman who looked like Mrs Thatcher.

But it worked.

As luck would have it my personal embarrassment, strict diet and rigid routine paid off.

Something clicked.

My super charged sperm swam it's way to the target.

On October 3rd 2000 Lucy was born.

I was the happiest bloke on the planet. I had two lovely sons and a beautiful daughter.

What more could a man want?

How about a faithful wife?

I'd always wanted a daughter who would grow up to be a "Daddy's Girl" who I could spoil rotten and treat like a little Princess.

It wasn't to be.

My ex-wife has stopped me from seeing my daughter since November 2008.

I can't and won't deny Julie was the love of my life.

Truth and loyalty have always been the character traits I admire most.

That is why everything I've written so far and will go on to write is the truth, the whole truth and nothing but the truth.

I will not edit my emotions to make me look like some so-called 'real man'.

I have and always will wear my heart on my sleeve.

I thought meeting her was the luckiest day of my life, for 15 years it was.

The time we spent together were the happiest times of my life and losing her the saddest.

The truth is, if I could make love to one woman for the rest of my life it would be Julie.

I fancy Kate Moss, Amanda Holden and Ola Jordan, but the love of my life was and always will be the mother of my three children.

Does that make me sound like a soft sentimental romantic and a wimp?

If it does, so what.

I'm no fan of fake news and will not re-write history to change the facts.

I honestly believe that if it hadn't been for her interfering parents and her infatuation with a self-confessed child abuser that we'd still be together.

And my three children would have grown-up with both a mum and a dad.

Life after Adultery

When I first met Julie I virtually gave up my daily use of fast drugs, but such is my personality, I swapped one addiction for another.

I have always needed a crutch. I'm sure it has something to do with my dad walking out on me when I was 13.

But more of that later.

I'm probably wrong but honestly don't believe amphetamines or cocaine did me any harm.

I loved the buzz I got from speed and the kick of cocaine. It made me tick and seemed to lift my IQ.

It didn't just help me to party or chat-up girls it gave me the ability to write.

Fast drugs did for me what LSD did for The Beatles and Ecstasy did for The Stone Roses.

There was also another reason I took fast drugs, which had nothing to do with being a 24-hour party person.

They kept me skinny.

The less I weighed the better I looked.

Just like catwalk models, jockeys, dancers and David Bowie I took stimulants because I wanted to be skinny.

The smaller my waist and more sunken my cheekbones the more girls I got.

I have one of those faces that don't do flesh.

At first my feelings for Julie replace my lust for life, for a while the party animal in me became extinct.

The irony is drink and drugs didn't destroy me. I was almost destroyed by the woman I loved.

I was betrayed by my soul mate and so hurt that on Christmas Eve I wrote a suicide note.

Not a lot of people know this but the song `Heartbreak Hotel` immortalised by Elvis Presley, started life as a suicide note.

My suicide note was not a cry for help. At the time I was genuinely up for doing it.

I was on my own and wouldn't have been found for days.

I lined up the tablets, wrote my `goodbye letters`, but it`s obvious I didn't go through with it.

I didn't bottle it.

I really didn't.

I stopped not because I think suicide is a coward`s way out.

I don't think it`s brave either.

Suicide can be painless to the person taking his or her life, but to those left behind it`s the most painful thing in the world.

It`s the cruellest act that one person can do to another.

I stopped myself because it`s so final.

You can`t change your mind half-way or come back from the dead.

I chose to live because I couldn't stop thinking about my three children.

I knew if I went through with it I`d be letting them down and giving my ex-wife and her parents the best Christmas present they`d ever had.

My survival instinct kicked in and I refused to grant Julie and her family their Christmas wish.

They had prayed for my death and shouted in the street at my sons "we hope your dad dies".

By taking my own life I would be playing into their hands.

If I had committed suicide, imagine all the lies they would have told my children about me?

They would have crucified my good name and dead men can`t talk or defend their reputation.

My ex-wife and her gloating family would have loved metaphorically stabbing a dead man in the back.

That reality check and concern for the safety of my 3 children pulled me back from the brink and inspired me to fight on.

What had made me so low?

The adultery of my ex-wife or the violent and sexual threats made to my children by her boyfriend?

It was a simple sentence made by a solicitor meant to be representing my interests.

I paid £500 to hear her say:

"You had better get used to seeing your children for 2 hours every Saturday and becoming a McDonalds Dad."

Adding:

"There is no way you will get custody"

My first reaction was to sack her, which I did, before slipping into the deepest depression imaginable.

It was the lowest moment of my entire life.

I had been a house-husband who`d taken his kids to school, attended every parents evening and Sports Day.

Every day I played football with my boys and took them to school.

We played board games, snooker, wrestled, boxed, dressed up as Action Men and bonded like super-glue.

And before she was taken from me had a close and special relationship with my daughter.

We didn`t play football but I walked her to Playschool, pushed her on the swings and took her on bus rides.

Lucy loved going on buses.

I got so much pleasure from being with them, sharing their company and making them laugh.

I enjoyed nothing more than taking them to the pictures or for a day-out at the seaside.

We saw Toy Story, Shrek, Stuart Little, One Hundred And One Dalmatians.

A different movie almost every week, but looking back Julie rarely came with us.

It was always the children and me.

Julie would come to Pantomimes, but Saturday afternoons at the movies were not her thing.

I was a `house-husband` and `primary carer` who loved every minute of it.

I was also a `bloody great Dad` who genuinely worshipped his children.

Being a dad was the best job in the world, so gave up the career I loved to be with them 24/7.

I had been there for them every single day for 12 years yet some snotty nosed, middle-class bitch tells me I am going to lose my children.

According to this woman I would no longer play a major role in their lives.

And why?

It wasn't me who'd been having a 10-month adulterous affair with a self-confessed child abuser.

My youngest son didn't walk-in on me in the lounge half-naked and having sex with Richard Grimson.

I didn't beat my eldest son so bad that his back was covered in red marks and bruises.

My ex-wife was as the Divorce Judgement and an Essex Social Services report confirm 'Guilty' of all the above.

So why should I lose my children?

According to the female solicitor it was because of my sex.

She said:

"The courts always believe that children are better off with their mother.

So, if I was you I'd get used to just seeing them for 2 hours every Saturday".

I was I admit in pieces for quite a while but never completely broken.

Though almost.

My decline was rapid and went from heartbroken to contemplating suicide.

The children were my world and had been since they were born in 1992, 1994 and the year 2000.

I could not face life without them.

It seemed suicide was my only option and the perfect alternative to losing them.

My character, personality, DNA or whatever you want to call it does not cope with losing people I genuinely love.

That is why I find it hard to let people get close in case they hurt me.

It's a fact of life that only those you love can hurt you.

I mentioned my Dad earlier and the truth is I never got over him walking out on me.

I survived but never came to terms with him leaving.

Even now part of me is still the 13-year-old boy he walked out on.

It made me the adult I became who was always scared of letting his guard down and falling in love.

In my life I have genuinely only loved 5 people and two of those betrayed me.

My dad and my ex-wife.

I always wanted to be the opposite of my dad and decided I was going to fight for my children.

I would take on the establishment and go to war with the Family Courts, Social Services and my ex-wife.

The truth is I have never been a quitter and decided to do what I do best.

Fight for justice.

All my life I've supported the underdog and challenged authority.

This was going to be my biggest fight. The odds were stacked against me.

It was Garry Johnson versus the world.

A devoted dad against the corrupt and biased world of family courts and Nazi-style social workers.

A war of attrition that almost killed me.

It didn't because of who I am and what I'm made of.

Much to the annoyance of Essex Social Services, my ex-wife and her parents I refused to die.

Social Worker Peter Brown told my sons "we wish your dad would disappear."

Adding:

"It would be so much easier without him being around".

What did he mean?

I knew what my ex-wife and former mother-in-law were thinking.

There was no mystery when they spotted Sam in the street and both shouted:

"We hope your dad dies".

At different times my ex-wife accused me of being a serial killer, a pornographer, mentally ill, a bad dad, mad, bad and dangerous and a male chauvinist.

What else could Julie make-up?

She told Social Services I was a suicide risk.

What I'm about to write sounds far-fetched but documents confirm it is fact.

As can my sons.

Sam and Adam were both taken out of their classrooms by Peter Brown and told:

"One day you could get home from school and find your dad hanging from a rope."

Thank God because my sons knew me so well they were not upset or distressed.

I was furious and the school agreed that next time Mr Brown turned up to interview the boys he could only see them if a teacher was present

It was Judge Moloney who made the most accurate statement.

He told Essex Social Services:

"Mr Johnson is like a dog with a bone and will not go away".

How right he was, the learned Judge had summed me up perfectly.

I was going nowhere and no matter how many times they knocked me down I would always get straight back up smiling and fighting.

I had right on my side and fought with every fibre in my being to get justice.

The morning after my darkest hour when I stared suicide in the face and my demons blinked.

I started the fightback.

That morning I said to myself:

"Sorry to disappoint you Julie Johnson and the Taylor family but I`m going nowhere.

You won`t be getting rid of me that easy".

My ex-wife and her parents would love to dance on my grave but they won`t get the chance.

I`m determined to live at least one day longer than the three of them.

Over a manic 24-hour period I transformed my `suicide note` and `Goodbye cruel world` letter into a battle plan.

I can`t explain my road to Damascus moment.

I can only guess that on Christmas Eve, when most people had a visit from Santa, I had a close encounter with the ghost of my Grandad.

He was a genuine Cockney and East End hard man who fought injustice all his life.

A Working class hero who fought against Sir Oswald Mosley and his Nazi Blackshirts.

His visit inspired me to fight on.

I metaphorically cried myself to sleep, but woke up Christmas morning with a smile on my face.

I wasn't grinning like a Cheshire cat, but I was no longer suicidal.

The previous year I'd woken up beside a warm naked body, a beautiful blonde with a heart of gold and a bum that most women would die for.

The house was full of noise as our three kids called for us to watch them open their presents.

On the morning of 2007, I woke up in a cold bed and the house was silent and empty.

It was now just a house and not a home.

There was no laughter, and for the first time in my life I was alone on Christmas morning.

It was bleak house in a Modern day setting, but even Dickens don't write them as dark as this.

A recovering would-be suicide statistic was singing the Christmas classic `Fairytale of New York` to his pet dog.

Oh, how the mighty fall.

I was home alone because the boys were hiding at a safe house.

Sam and Adam were on the run from Social Services, the Police and Julie.

They'd spent 3 weeks staying at 11 secret addresses all over Essex, Kent and South London.

One night they stayed at a safe house in Hertfordshire, just yards from the EastEnders studio.

At times it was like being in a movie as they were taken to railway stations, McDonald's drive-ins and multi-story car parks and were transferred from one car to another.

We were always one step ahead of the authorities.

I'd always been a risk taker, broken the rules (mostly for the hell of it), but since becoming a single parent, I'd learnt how to be a `rebel with a cause` rather than for the sake of it.

This time I had right on my side and the moral high-ground.

The Fight Goes On

I would like to officially put on-the-record that before she started sleeping around and left with our daughter in July 2005, Julie was the perfect wife.

A wonderful loving mum during the day and at night a whore in the bedroom.

I had the best of both worlds. What more could a man want?

She had 2 sides to her character which I found attractive.

In company she was sweet, well-mannered and at times almost shy.

Apart from our Wedding Day I don't think we ever kissed in front of her parents.

But in private she was up for everything. There was nothing she would not try at least once.

This is why in the 15 years we were together I never even looked at another woman.

I was one hundred per cent faithful and despite everything for the first 14 years still believe she was.

We differed politically as I was an anarchist whereas she was a bit of a Tory.

And although not a Royalist she did love Lady Di.

We disagreed about politics but united in our hatred of child killers like Ian Huntley, Myra Hindley and Roy Whiting.

We both hated any form of child abuse

Together we shouted at the telly when Huntley was arrested during a live SKY TV broadcast.

This is one of the reasons I was so hurt and angry at her choice of boyfriend.

The Julie I knew would never have allowed a pervert anywhere near our children.

I know that for a fact.

So how could she defend a man who verbally sexually abused and violently threatened her own flesh and blood?

A pervert who admitted his vile behavior to the police.

Essex social worker Peter Brown said: "Mrs Johnson admits she knows all about his threats, but doesn't understand why you keep mentioning it".

Adding:

"Why are you so obsessed about it?"

For those doubting the content of the previous paragraph, her acknowledgement of his vile behavior appears in official Essex Social Services documents.

The paperwork I obtained by going to The High Court and using the Freedom of Information Act.

Judge Newton also commented on the verbal sexual abuse and violent threats saying:

"I have spoken with Sam and not for one moment do I doubt what he told me"

He added:

"And the fact is Mr Grimson admitted his behavior to the police.

It's my opinion that he spoke to Sam in a most disgraceful manner".

Adding:

"It is never helpful when a third party is involved"

He also rebuked my ex-wife for not speaking out about the vile behavior of her boyfriend saying:

"Mrs Johnson should acknowledge the facts and address this matter as both boys are entitled to hear that their mother believes them"

The quotes you have just read I not only personally heard the Judge say but they also appeared in the official court document.

Essex Social Services behaved just like the social workers in the North of England who covered-up the vile behavior of the grooming gangs.

It would take 8 years for Helen Lincoln, the Head of Essex Social Services to admit the many mistakes of her department.

She confirmed in writing that the behavior of Richard Grimson and the attacks on my children had not been properly investigated.

Yes, it took that long but I never gave up, as Judge Moloney warned Essex Social Services:

"Mr Johnson is like a dog with a bone and will not go away".

But at the time Essex Social Services and Peter Brown in particular were not interested in the truth.

I had told them everything and provided proof as had Sam and Adam.

The police even confirmed her boyfriend's guilt but Social Services turned a deaf ear.

They were determined whatever the danger that both boys would live with Mrs Johnson.

Social workers had no interest in the safety of my children.

Not just mine, but kids in general.

They knew thousands of young girls were being gang raped in northern towns and covered it up for decades.

How many news reports have you seen on TV where a child supposedly under the care of Social Services has been murdered by a stepfather?

But whatever the threats of social worker Peter Brown Sam and Adam were not interested in playing pretend `happy families` with Mrs Johnson and her boyfriend.

It just wasn't going to happen, not then, not ever, and hasn't happened at any time in the past 13 years.

But Essex Social Services were confident of snatching both boys from my care and forcing them to live with my ex-wife and her boyfriend.

Peter Brown would issue threats and boast:

"We never lose. I have personally never lost a case".

Adding:

"You don't realise how powerful I am Mr Johnson".

He then issued a sinister threat hoping it would scare the boys back into the arms of Mr Johnson.

Saying:

"If you don't persuade the boys to co-operate we'll have them locked-up in a secure unit".

I know what you are thinking.

I'm lying and things like that don't happen in a so-called democratic country like the United Kingdom.

I can assure you they do and have the official documents that prove it.

I went to The High Court where Essex Social Services were ordered to handover all the files.

I have in my possession a document which states:

"Mrs Johnson wants both boys sent to a secure unit in Cambridgeshire".

I hope you agree that this was a disgusting request.

The Detention Centre was more then 100 miles away from Wickford.

Sam and Adam had committed no crime. They`d not been found `guilty` of any crime.

What was illegal in wanting to live with their dad?

It was hardly the crime of the century.

Social worker Peter Brown was like a German soldier at the end of World War Two.

He was claiming he was only following orders.

The Fuhrer in our war didn`t have a silly moustache she had long blonde hair.

Julie Johnson was calling the shots and Peter Brown was happy to play along.

They used every dirty trick in the book.

Brown was her chief spin doctor whose job was to blacken my name at every opportunity.

When it came to spreading fake news and false facts he was in the same league as Lord Haw Haw.

Brown like Tony Blair could produce dodgy documents in his sleep.

He spread more muck than a pig farmer.

It all got very personal.

He accused me of being a member of the Murdoch press saying:

"Mrs Johnson tells me you're a tabloid journalist.

Do you work for Rupert Murdoch"?

I replied:

"Yes I`m Editor of The Sun".

He was not amused as Social workers have no sense of humor.

He said:

"I was on the Wapping picket line every day".

I replied:

"I remember seeing you on News At Ten with Arthur Scargill."

This flippant remark was met with silence.

I added:

"I was a Freelance music journalist. I worked for lots of people".

Brown:

"If you worked for The Sun you must be a Tory".

I thought where is this going?

I soon found out.

Brown said:

"I still support the SWP. I hate The Sun and anyone who works for Murdoch".

It was bizarre as here was a middle-class posh boy, a suburban rebel, a weekend warrior having a pop at a genuine Working class rebel and punk poet.

I replied:

"Like I said I was a Freelance journalist.

I worked for Sounds music magazine and sold showbiz stories to The Sun, Daily Mirror, The Sunday People, News of The World, Daily Star, Evening Standard and The Daily Record in Scotland.

So, what?"

Adding:

"Does that make me Kelvin McKenzie?"

After that bizarre encounter no meeting ever took place without Brown describing me as a Sun journalist.

Next, he accused me of being a Tory.

They say there has to be a first time for everything in your life.

I wasn`t and never will be a Conservative voter or supporter.

What did any of this have to do with my ability to be a great Dad?

The Social Worker sneered:

"Mrs Johnson told me you stood as Conservative candidate and have brainwashed the boys to be Tories".

Sam and Adam were 13 and 11 with no interest in politics.

I was a life-long rebel who`d always believed in the abolition of the Royal Family and The House of Lords.

What kind of Tory could I possibly be?

I was sitting in my own house and being accused of brainwashing my kids into becoming Tories.

To quote Richard Littlejohn:

"You couldn`t make it up".

Brown added:

"Mrs Johnson has shown us a leaflet."

I replied;

"I don't know what it's got to do with you, but I'll tell you what happened.

I was out with the kids walking the dog and spotted this bloke knocking on doors.

It was just before the 1997 local elections and he was a Tory foot soldier.

The boys asked what he was doing and for a laugh I said, `wait until he knocks at ours`.

I got Sam and Adam to answer the door.

I followed trying not to laugh and to cut a long story short told the bloke I was a Tory.

I was so convincing. I've always had the gift of the gab and he asked me to be a candidate.

A few days later he turns up with a form which he asks me to sign.

It was a nomination paper and asks me to write down a few of my personal thoughts.

He wants them for an election leaflet.

I promised to email him.

I wrote:

"Vote for me and I'll campaign to abolish the Royal Family and The House of Lords".

I don't think he agreed because I wasn't asked to join the Conservative party.

At the time I thought it was hilarious and so did Julie.

She joked: "If you get elected I'll buy a hat".

The boys still laugh about it and one of us will mention it whenever there's General Election coverage on TV.

This political smear highlights just how dangerous and gullible Peter Brown really was.

He never checked his facts and believed whatever outrageous lies my ex-wife told him.

It's true what they say "power corrupts" and like the current President of the United States Julie was deluded.

She genuinely believed people would always believe whatever lies she told about me.

My ex-wife was losing the plot and her arrogance was spiraling out of control.

This led to Julie scoring an amazing own goal which destroyed her reputation.

She thought she could expose me as a porn movie-maker without revealing it was her who starred in the films.

I don't know who was advising her or whether it was solely down to her.

But the whole episode was bizarre.

She'd already `outed` herself in open court and was now having a second bite of the cherry.

What was it that Goebbels said?

"If you tell the same lie enough times people will start to believe it".

It was surely a legal first.

Julie was at the same time both the instigator and victim of `revenge porn`.

It was the biggest own goal since Roy of the Rovers put the ball in his own net playing against Manchester United.

The irony is had she not attempted to stitch me up her career in adult movies would have remained a secret.

When that failed she told Social Services I had a history of mental illness.

Once again Peter Brown fell for her fabricated story hook, line and sinker.

He gave gullible peop a bad name.

Had Julie told him the earth was flat and Father Christmas lived on the moon he'd have believed her.

The truth is I saw a counsellor for stress and not a mental health problem.

In 2000 and 2002 the papers and TV news were full of stories about missing children.

The murders of 2 friends Holly & Jessica and Sarah Payne.

I was already a over anxious parent worrying about the safety of his kids.

The high-profile murders coincided with Sam and Adam wanting to visit the park on their own.

They wanted to be with their mates so reluctantly I had to agree.

It freaked me out.

I was such a nervous wreck I would follow behind on the other side of the road.

The dog was worn out.

My GP put me medication to calm my nerves and not because I was mentally ill.

Serial Killer

I was becoming increasingly frustrated because despite numerous run-ins with Social Services, the police, The CMHT and the DSS.

I was still not getting the opportunity to put my side of the story.

Every day I thought how long would it be before I have my day in court?

Unbeknown to me there had already been three court Hearings, all held in secret with my solicitors ordered not to inform me.

Talk about `what a load of bollocks` it is when UK politicians boast on TV that British Justice is the best in the world.

My own legal team were gagged from informing me about the secret Proceedings and threatened with contempt of court if they did.

It all happened behind closed doors in a setting reminiscent of War Trials in Nazi Germany or Soviet Russia.

The press was excluded as were members of the public.

What did they have to hide?

It was not a fair fight. It was like Mike Tyson fighting a man with no arms.

It was like West Ham playing a match behind closed doors against a team with no players.

The secret Hearings resulted in me being sent to a Maximum security prison and classified as `mad, bad and dangerous`.

A mentally ill and potential serial killer.

There had been no trial.

I had no opportunity to defend myself and was found "guilty" in my absence.

My wife had been allowed to make false allegations in secret without producing a shred of evidence.

As stated earlier I was examined at Bellmarsh Prison found to be 100 per cent sane and returned to a hero`s welcome from my sons.

From now on I attended every court Hearing at Southend, Chelmsford, Colchester, Basildon, Cambridge, Romford and finally The High Court in London.

I went through 3 teams of solicitors and 2 barristers before representing myself.

I was also helped by two members of Parliament and my case was taken up on the floor of The House of Commons.

My plight was featured in Hansard the official parliamentary diary.

Before my first appearance at Southend I`d already seen off the RSPCA.

My ex-wife reported I was neglecting a cat. I didn't even own a cat.

I was then visited by the Environmental Health Team from Basildon Council.

My ex-wife had reported my sons were living in a house full of rats.

Next up was the fraud department of the DSS.

This was the second time I`d been reported for swindling the government.

I`d now been accused of Child benefit and Housing Benefit fraud.

Two guys in suits were standing on my doorstep.

They claimed my ex-wife had informed them I was working illegally.

Once again I proved my innocence.

This was followed by more visits from Social Services and the police trying to take my sons.

I was desperate for my day in court.

I wanted the chance to defend myself and prove I wasn`t a bad dad.

I was ready to answer the questions I expected to hear.

The court was packed with middle-class professionals reveling in their positions of power.

A combination of self-important jumped up little Hitler`s and Maggie Thatcher impersonators.

I wasn't prepared for what was about to happen.

I`d been accused at an ex-parte Hearing of being mentally ill and a serial killer with a Hit List.

Now to my face I was once again Garry Johnson the porn producer.

The guy with the mental health problems.

I'd already dealt with this and proved I wasn`t `mentally ill` or a `Serial Killer`.

I`d already admitted to making porn films with Julie Johnson.

I`d explained how I`d been treated for stress.

So why was she bringing it all up again?

As before the allegations were deliberately vague.

There was no description of what type of porn my ex-wife was talking about?

I was genuinely worried.

I did not want those judging me to think I was some kind of pervert.

How did they know about my hobby?

I soon found out.

The usher handed me a document which stated "Julie Johnson wants the return of her 4 pornographic films and 70 pornographic pictures".

I was puzzled.

Why was she once again putting her acting and modelling into the public domain?

Why did she only ask for 4 of the films?

Julie had already `outed` herself in open court so why involve Service Services and Cafcass?

There was no limit to the dirty tricks she`d pull too gain custody of my children?

It was her intention to give the false impression I`d forced her into making pornographic films.

I wasn't wrong.

It`s exactly what she told Cafcass and Social Worker Peter Brown.

I didn't want to do repeat what I`d already said in court but was fighting to keep my boys.

I had no choice.

I was trying hard to protect my reputation.

I reluctantly admitted to making pornographic films between 1992 and 2004.

I had to reveal Julie starred in all 34 films.

I explained that at no time did I ever force her to take part.

I wasn't happy re-living and repeating what I`d said before but had no choice.

I know how Social Services and Cafcass think.

If I'd said "no comment" and refused to talk I'd be accused of having something to hide.

I had to speak out as Julie had left me with no choice.

This time I didn't hold back,

I made sure people were in no doubt about the content.

I was no pervert and the films were not perverted.

No way was I staying silent and letting people get the wrong impression.

I was no pervert and the films were not perverted. They involved 2 consenting adults having sex.

Julie would dress up in sexy outfits and strip off.

There be plenty of role-playing with Julie pretending to be everything from an escort to a stripper.

I insisted that she liked performing as much as I enjoyed filming and directing them.

I hoped by being so open and graphic the subject would never be mentioned again.

I heard no more from Cafcass but Social Services wouldn't let it go.

Peter Brown was determined to hang me out to dry.

He knocked on my door with a fresh allegation saying:

"Mrs Johnson claims you sent pornographic pictures to her place of work".

I replied:

"She said this last year".

Brown:

"She's talking about last week".

I assured him I did not send any pictures and asked if he'd seen them. He hadn't.

I suggested he asks to see them and then hands them over to the police for examination.

They can look for fingerprints and trace the camera.

He approached my ex-wife who again could not hand over any photographs.

She claimed her boss had ripped them up and thrown them in the bin.

I'm not a born sceptic but haven't we heard this before?

What sort of idiot destroys the evidence?

Or maybe just a suggestion, there wasn't any evidence to destroy.

I'm still not happy about being 'outed' as a porno movie-maker, in case some people think I did put pressure on my ex-wife to make them.

Whatever the facts people like Peter Brown always think "there is no smoke without fire".

I can assure you it is not true and will explain why throughout our marriage Julie and I made pornographic films.

It was because role-playing meant we didn't have to cheat or look for other partners.

It was my idea to start with. It was selfish on my part but not for the reasons you are thinking.

It had nothing to do with power or taking advantage. It was all about having a happy and lasting marriage.

I suggested making movies because I was scared of losing my wife and being unfaithful.

I had never been faithful in my life because I always got bored and fancied a change.

We'd been together 3 years and I came up with the idea of her dressing up, wearing different coloured wigs and pretending to be someone else.

She not only agreed but came with me to buy the video camera.

We spent £750 in Dixons on the A127.

I was so excited in the shop Julie laughed at the bulge in my boxers.

I couldn't wait to get home and start filming. That night she made her debut as 'Linda Lovelace' with me in the role of Ben Dover.

She showered, blow dried her hair and climbed into a black open-crotch body stocking.

She looked stunning and the rest I will leave to your imagination.

I won't reveal any more magic moments but must for the sake of my reputation give a factual account of Julie's involvement.

Not concerning sexual content but by revealing her participation in the productions.

It was always a joint effort.

We chose outfits together in Anne Summers shops and bought various wigs from The Gallery at Lakeside.

Julie got her St Trinians costume from a school shop on Canvey Island.

The mention of Canvey Island reminds me of an incident that reveals both her personality and love of porn.

We were watching a Channel 4 documentary in around 1999/2000 about Lee Anne McQueen a porn actress from Canvey Island.

It was uncanny as from the neck down without her clothes on they were identical.

Julie could have been her body double though she was twice as good-looking with much better hair.

McQueen was dark-haired and Julie was blonde

The program interested us because Canvey was only a couple of miles from Pitsea.

Julie went on for weeks about how she was `sexier` and a `better actress`.

She was.

The truth is and the camera doesn`t lie. The films she made were far superior to those of her Canvey rival.

They were filmed at different locations over a 12-year period and feature Julie with a variety of hairstyles and different body shapes.

A size 8 before she had two children and a size 10 after she`d had three.

I point this out not in my role as a movie critic but because it contradicts the lies she told Social Worker Peter Brown.

Julie told the Court, the police and Social Services she only made 4 and that I forced her to appear.

I did not force her to pose for pornographic Polaroid pictures or to appear in 4 pornographic films.

The truth is over a 12-year period she willingly starred in 34 adult movies shot at various Essex locations

The different décor and furnishings in the lounges and bedrooms of 11 Shirley Gardens, 30 The Gables, 64 Chestnut Road and 22 Bridge Road confirm that fact.

Those are the 4 properties we lived at between 1991 and 2005.

If Julie Johnson had not attempted to discredit me in a Southend Courtroom the world would never have known about our secret hobby.

My last word on the subject.

Julie did have a porn star double. They are/were so alike it`s as if they were separated at birth.

The adult actress she most resembled was Brighton beauty Melissa Walker.

In 2003 the blonde stunner was splashed all over the tabloids for stabbing her lover.

She was high on coke and found guilty of attempted murder and it ended her movie career.

The first time I saw her picture in the paper I genuinely thought it was Julie.

She was a stunner as was my ex-wife.

A few months after the drama of Southend Court the show moved to Chelmsford.

This time Julie Johnson claimed I was stopping Sam and Adam from seeing her and was supported by Social Worker Peter Brown.

Their decision had nothing to do with me and at long last I was allowed to explain why they'd disowned their mum.

What I'm about to say is accepted as fact by every legal document and the police.

The factual claims also appear in the Essex Social Services documents I obtained after going to The High Court.

This is why my sons stopped talking to my ex-wife in 2005 and to this day still don't.

Adam walked in on his mum half-naked and having sex with her boyfriend in the lounge of 22 Bridge Road Wickford.

He was 10 years old.

Sam doesn't talk to his mum not just because of what Adam told him but because she beat him black and blue.

She hit him so hard his back was covered in red marks and bruises.

Injuries he showed to both his teacher and football trainer.

He was 12 years old.

In 2005 both boys disowned their mum because she allowed her boyfriend to violently threaten and verbally sexually abuse them.

The worst of numerous incidents were as followed.

A phone call to Sam where her boyfriend says, and I'm quoting word for word.

"I am the bloke whose fucking your mum, she's here with me now, so is your sister Lucy and I'm taking pictures. Do you want to see them?"

Adding:

"I'm the man whose fucking your sister".

165

There were 14 calls in total

That vile abuse was accepted as fact in various courts and by Basildon Police.

Julie refused to believe and called both boys "lying little shits" adding "Richard said he didn't and I believe him".

Grimson admitted his perverted behaviour but she still sided with him against her own sons.

A point picked up by the Judge but ignored by Social Services.

That is why both boys refused to see her.

Her boyfriend also threatened both boys with an iron bar shouting and swearing:

"I'm going to fucking do you".

This is why both boys still refuse to see her.

There were many more threats and incidents but Julie continued to put her feelings for her boyfriend before her own flesh and blood.

Both boys have not spoken to their mum since 2005.

I explained to the Court I had no advanced warning that Julie was planning to leave.

I was only Adam catching her 'in the act' that alerted me to her affair.

I didn't have a clue.

It was only after Julie left that Adam revealed more details.

He had twice seen her kissing Southend football trainer Ian Fleming.

Julie swapped her children for a pervert with no brains, no morals and no front teeth there had been no bust up, previous split or separation of any kind.

Everything seemed quite normal when she went away on a family holiday with our three children and her parents 2 weeks before she left.

At the time I had no idea about her fling with Fleming and affair with Grimson.

If I had known anything about her cheating, would I have paid for the holiday?

A family holiday I couldn't afford and wasn't well enough to go on.

I often wonder was it during those 14 days in the company of her pond-life parents that she decided to break-up the family.

It was a fortnight in Spain where whenever she was on the phone told both boys to go away.

It's only with hindsight that I can see Julie came back a different person.

The woman who swaggered into 22 Bridge Road was not the cute and cheerful Julie who went on holiday.

She returned foul-mouthed and mini-skirted.

At the time I thought too much sun and too many Southern Comforts was responsible for her cheap chav 'new look'.

Julie had morphed into 'Ginger' her skanky best friend with footballer's legs.

Did she have something on her mind? Would she have left even if Adam hadn't of 'caught her in the act'?

She had a vacant expression and had shed every shred of her personality. It was like looking at a 'female version' of her mother.

Something major had happened.

She was like a zombie.

They do say 'daughters always end up like their mothers", well God help Lucy, that's all I can say.

I want to clarify that by saying 'I only mean the Julie after the summer 2005'.

So, what changed Julie?

Who persuaded her to walk out on her family?

Her mother, Richard Grimson or best friend 'Ginger'?

All three got inside her head but the leader of the gang was her hard-faced, foul-mouthed friend 'Ginger'.

An ugly woman both inside and out who'd been waiting 15 years to pounce.

'Ginger' was a bitter woman who looked like a down-market version of Coronation Street character Liz McDonald.

Her own husband had just left her so maybe she was jealous of Julie.

'Ginger' was a woman on her own who maybe coped with her own separation by encouraging Julie to dump her family.

Unbeknown to me at the time 'Ginger' was providing alibis so my ex-wife could meet Grimson.

In the years that followed 'Ginger' would rant and rave at my sons and brainwash my daughter against me.

She told anyone who would listen including Peter Brown that I was a `bad dad`.

This from women I`d only met about 10 times in 15 years.

In the crazy world of Peter Brown this made her an expert witness.

Social Services refused to speak to any member of my family or interview a single friend.

The bias was unbelievable. As far as they were concerned it was an open and shut case.

Julie Johnson was innocent and I was guilty of everything from the troubles in Northern Ireland to the Iraq War.

If Peter Brown had his way I`d be arrested for the murders of JFK and Martin Luther King.

When Julie and the boys returned from holiday there were still Seven days to go before I found out about her affair.

The car pulled up and our three children run up the path to kiss and cuddle me.

I approached Julie and got a kiss a father would give his daughter.

It was friendly but minus any passion.

Julie chose to sleep in the spare room claiming she felt sick and tired.

The day before she jetted off on holiday we had a `quickie` on the sofa.

I know I was too quick, but in my defence I was having health problems.

My medication hadn`t `kicked in`.

Medical experts blame it on `poor blood flow`. It`s the early sign of a heart condition.

Our final sexual act wasn't romantic, erotic or much to boast about either.

It was the day before she left to be with Richard Grimson.

After 15 years passion, dirty sex, all sorts of fun and games it was all over in a minute.

The final act of intimacy was a blow-job next to an ironing board in a room full of washing.

There was no kissing and immediately afterwards she returned to the ironing.

It was a cold and horrible way to say "goodbye" to a woman I`d loved for 15 years.

That was it, the end, the last hurrah, our final sexual encounter and she left the next day.

In a way I'd had a lucky escape as years later a copy of her medical report found its way into my Legal Bundle.

Julie can't deny this as I have a copy of the document and Dr Sohota wouldn't lie.

He'd been treating her for a STD in December 2004 at the same time I wasn't sleeping with her and both Grimson and Fleming were.

There was another interesting fact in the same document obtained by my solicitor.

Why was Julie was having Depo-Prevaro birth control injections between November 2004 and June 2005?

She wasn't having sex with me!

It was not me who gave her the STD and it wasn't me who got her pregnant.

Her medical records reveal Julie had no history of birth control injections or of sexually transmitted diseases.

Julie would now be out of my life forever, or so I thought.

We never spoke again but she would soon launch a campaign of lies, false allegations and harassment.

Julie was the `guilty` party yet behaving like a woman scorned.

We Are a Family

It was a sunny Saturday afternoon and I was at a school fete with Adam and Lucy.

Apart from my occasional chest pains and money worries I didn't have a care in the world.

I'd always coped with life by ignoring anything that was sad or serious.

I only did happy and upbeat as life is too short to waste time on negatives.

The three of us had a great time. As always Adam had a football under his arm and Lucy was riding her 3-wheel bike.

At around 4, earlier than planned and Julie expected we left for home.

Adam run ahead and I lagged behind with Lucy as she was no Bradley Wiggins on her bike.

We were about 500 yards behind him.

Then running as fast as he could Adam came speeding towards us.

His tan had disappeared and he was as white as a ghost.

What had happened?

I would soon find out.

Adam had walked in on his mum half-naked and `at it` in the lounge with her boyfriend.

He was badly shaken and I was stunned.

My first thought was to go steaming in but had to comfort Adam and couldn't leave Lucy alone in the street.

What should only have been a 3-minute walk took ages as I had to carry both my daughter and her bike.

On our arrival the house was empty.

As I was looking around I heard Sam shouting out `Dad`.

He was storming about shouting and swearing as his brother had told him everything.

Both boys without a word from me were instantly united in their hatred for Julie.

I was still in a state of shock and unable to get my head around what had happened.

But I already knew and accepted we were finished. It is not in my DNA to forgive betrayal.

That evening Julie returned and `no` I didn't hit her or even threaten too.

And the only raised voice was hers.

I don`t believe in violence against women, children or bullying of any kind.

I didn't say a word as I`ve got a rule to never speak to people I don`t like.

As I told my children life is too short so why waste time arguing.

I did though I admit give her the dirtiest of dirty looks but never said a word.

Julie didn't just return to pack her bags and go. She expected the children to leave with her.

She told Sam, Adam and Lucy to line up against the wall in the lounge.

Both boys ignored her. Instead staring at her with hate in their eyes and hurt in their hearts.

Julie said:

"I`m leaving and you`re coming with me".

When both boys said:

"We`re staying with our Dad", she went ballistic, shouting, swearing and then exploding into violence.

She completely lost the plot and screamed at them:

"He sees me naked, he fucks me and you two had better get used to it".

Julie then flew at Sam in a mad rage striking him across the face, punching and slapping him about the body.

When I intervened she slapped me across the face so hard my dark glasses went flying across the room.

Some of her punches led to Sam having red marks and bruising on his back for days.

Not re-writing history as this incident was reported to the police and Sam showed the bruises to his Head of Year and football trainer.

The last time Sam was touched by his mum it was not a kiss or a cuddle.

It was a clenched fist.

Lucy was crying and clinging to Adam as my ex-wife continued to scream and shout.

My last words to my daughter as I removed her fingers from his shirt were:

"Come on babe, don`t cry, you have got to go with your mum".

I thought I was doing the right thing.

She was only five and had no idea I wouldn't see her again for almost two years.

Julie picked up my daughter and as she headed for the front door snarled:

"Don`t think you are keeping those boys".

She then spat in my face hoping to get a reaction but when that failed she left.

Despite her unreasonable behaviour and blatant provocation Social Services would always blame me for everything.

According to them Sam and Adam refusing to have contact with their mum was my fault.

They ignored the fact she beat Sam up and that Adam caught her `in the act` with her boyfriend.

Both boys had already disowned her months before the start of violent threats and verbal sexual abuse.

Her cheating didn't just betray me it destroyed many lives and as Julie would find out a lifetime of consequences.

Adultery breaks hearts and leaves scars that never heal.

I know that sounds dramatic and emotional but that is what happens when a parent walks out on their children.

I once was one of those children deserted by a parent and the pain has never left me.

Losing a parent is bad enough but it`s heart-breaking when it involves violence.

The natural instinct of a parent should be to protect your children at all times.

Whatever their age they should always be your number one priority.

From the day she left in July 2005 to now both boys have had no contact with Julie.

There would be no more Birthday, Christmas or Mother Day cards.

Julie paid a heavy price for walking out on her children to be with a self-confessed child abuser.

She got a life sentence with no remission, no parole or second chance.

Straight-forward adultery and a normal divorce is one thing but what happened next was not.

This explains why Sam and Adam stood-up to Social Services and ignored the orders of the Family Court.

A few weeks after Julie left a scruffy social worker turned up at my front door.

The visit was unannounced so I had no prior warning and this worked to my advantage.

This middle-class woman waived an ID card in my face and said:

"I`m from Essex Social Services"

Adding:

"Can I come in?"

I replied:

"Why"?

She said:

"Your wife claims that your children are under-nourished, not being fed and living in squalor.

This visit was not planned.

I had no advanced warning or any idea they were coming or that Social Services were out to get me.

I had nothing to hide so invited the lady in.

She asked to look around.

It was like an army inspection.

All she needed was a magnifying glass. She inspected both boy`s bedrooms and I`m talking inside wardrobes and under beds.

The woman even checked my bedroom, the bathroom and the laundry cupboard.

I could see the disappointment on her face when everything was found to be spotless.

She checked the lounge, dining room, kitchen, Conservatory and was far from happy to find them all neat and tidy.

I asked:

"Anything else?"

She replied "Oh yes Mr Johnson".

Adding:

"I want to inspect the content of the fridge, the freezer and the kitchen cupboards".

Me:

"Why?"

She sneered:

"Because according to Mrs Johnson you are not feeding the boys properly".

I was both fuming and smiling at the same time.

Angry because of the false allegation but extremely happy because I knew the contents.

I did the shopping.

My ex-wife had forgotten in her attempt to smear me that both boys trained 2 nights a week with a professional football club.

They ate a healthy diet by following a strict lifestyle sheet provided by the club.

The social worker found a kitchen full of chicken, tuna, pasta, fresh fruit and vegetables.

She was not happy and left in a huff but without a word of apology.

A month letter I received a letter from Essex Social Services which stated "No further action".

They`d forgotten to include an apology.

I would learn in the years to follow that Essex Social Services do not like saying "sorry".

I would have to fight for one. Put my life and liberty on the line to get any sort of apology.

It would be 2010 before I got a verbal `sorry` and 2013 before I got one in writing.

I loved being a dad and took to it like a duck to water.

I was without `blowing my own trumpet` pretty good at it.

I`d found my vocation in life, it was the first thing I had ever excelled at.

I screwed up at football, was a failed pop singer and an average showbiz writer.

I was also a `top dad`.

I loved everything about it from football in the park to Saturday afternoon at the movies.

I could not have survived the past 13 years without the love and support of my two boys.

They are both `chips off the old block` together we saw off Essex Social Services, the corrupt Family Courts and the police.

But being a single parent isn`t easy and I`m not just talking about shopping, cooking and housework.

A lovely lady helped me through the early days of my divorce.

She was extremely attractive in every way, funny and great company.

But, sadly she was also a married woman.

I fancied her like mad, and still do, but to me a married woman is always out of bounds.

I saw her every day but our relationship was more `brother and sister` than Romeo and Juliet.

But her husband didn`t see it that way and one day I got an irate phone call.

I perfectly understood as she was very pretty, slim and naturally blonde.

In fact one hundred per cent my type.

We stopped seeing each other and continued our `relationship` on the phone.

I dealt with a lot of my mixed emotions by reading `Thugs, Mugs and Violence`, a book by East End hard man Jamie O`Keefe.

It helped to sort out my head and see the positive side of things.

It was written by a guy who`d experienced the cheating wife syndrome, was half-Irish Cockney like me and had spent time in care.

He was also a single parent raising two sons. How spooky was that?

Luckily for Richard Grimson it was Jamie`s wise words that prevented him becoming a real-life corpse.

He said:

"Gal I`ve got mates doing 20 years in prison for 20 seconds of violence".

Adding:

"Don`t do anything silly".

Weeks before I had done something `very silly`. It was the one and only time I reverted to the wild ways of my teenage years.

But more of that later.

The hardest thing about being a single dad.

Apart from being `targeted` by jealous husbands, is the ironing and changing a duvet as I was terrible at both.

Sleeping alone is also strange as is watching all the TV programs you watched with your wife and talked/argued about.

We always clashed over The Bill as she supported the coppers and I sided with the criminals if they were working class or being fitted-up.

Listening to the radio is no fun either because they keep playing records you still think of as `our song`.

There is nobody to share your opinions with or to laugh at your jokes.

If it was hard for me to adjust, what must it have been like for Sam and Adam?

Their mum went off with another man and took their sister with her.

If that weren`t bad enough they also had to put up with my cooking.

Amazingly both boys came through it all unaffected and never mentioned their mother.

I cannot put into words how much I appreciated their 100 per cent loyalty.

They only got upset when her boyfriend threatened them or mother abused them in the street.

Parents of school friends would always tell me how both boys were coping.

I still remember the first Mother`s Day after she left.

Adam was asked by the mum of his best mate:

"What have you got your mum?"

To which he replied;

"I ain`t got a mum".

Another time the mother of Sam`s best friend revealed what he told her at the dinner table.

He said:

"She ain`t my mum and I never want to see her again?"

I was not present on either occasion, yet I was still accused by my ex-wife and Social Services of turning the both boys against her.

Nothing could be further from the truth.

I never badmouthed her because not once did I ever mention her name in the house.

As I told Social Worker Peter Brown:

"I never said anything nice and I never said anything nasty."

Adding:

"To me she is a non-person."

Yet I was still accused of brainwashing my sons as if I was the Wickford version of Paul McKenna.

God, if I had the gift of hypnotism I`d be appearing on TV and earning millions.

Unlike him I ain`t got `hypnotic powers` but I have got a full head of hair.

So, no way would I swap places with him.

In the underworld the saying goes:

"If you can`t do the time don't do the crime".

That is why at the very last minute I pulled out of committing the crime I mentioned earlier.

I didn't fancy 20 years behind bars.

Grimson had violently threatened and verbally sexually abused my 2 sons and people were telling me to do him.

I lost count of how many people said:

"If I was you I`d kill him".

It`s easy to say when you haven`t actually got to do it.

But the voices in your head grow louder and on one occasion I was tempted to do it.

A friend of a friend sent down 2 heavies from South-East London.

They arrived just before Adam got home from school and no lie one of them was almost 7ft tall.

So big he had to duck to get into the conservatory.

Adam was so impressed he went and got his mates so they could come in and see the jolly mean giant.

We drove to Grimson's home at 40 Hyde Way Wickford and parked across his drive, but luckily for him and on reflection for me too, he was out.

If he had been in I wouldn't be writing this book. I`d be in prison and halfway through a life sentence.

We both had a narrow escape.

Then a few days later her boyfriend verbally sexually abused my five-year-old daughter.

I wanted to blow his fucking legs off, throw acid in his face, or douse him in petrol and burn him alive.

A close friend was ex-army and still thought like a member of the SAS.

He staked out his house and was planning to kidnap him.

The plan was to bundle him into the back of a van, drive into the country and set fire to it.

Four of us sat in my lounge discussing this plan in great detail and came close to putting it into action.

I knew the trail would lead back to me and that I couldn't cope being away from Sam and Adam for 20 years.

There was then another incident which was so vile and disgusting I did something I had never done before.

I reported it to the police.

I didn't consider myself a grass as I was trying to legally protect my children.

February 8th 2006.

8pm.

I'd spent the day in Southend at the funeral of a very good friend and returned home around 6pm both shattered and emotional.

I am slumped in an armchair half-watching the TV with Sam and Adam.

The phone rings and is answered by 13-year-old Sam.

Once again he is threatened with violence and verbally sexually abused by the boyfriend of my ex-wife.

Tough `perverse talk` from a `plastic gangster` to a kid in the lower year of senior school.

Grimson must have thought he was still in the school playground bullying weaker kids.

He threatens to beat Sam up and again boasts that Lucy, his sister and my 5-year-old daughter is taking pictures of him having sex with his mum.

It gets a lot worse he claims he`s fucking Lucy.

He asks Sam if he wants to see the pictures.

His actual words were:

"Do you want to see pictures of me fucking your mum and sister?"

How sick is that?

Sam replies:

"You do know I`m only 13".

Grimson snarls:

"I don't care how fucking old you are I'm coming to your school to beat you up".

Sam was shaking and as white as a sheet as he informed me of the phone call.

This time I called the police.

I reported it to Social Services and sent an email to my former mother-in-law as I wanted this incident on-the-record.

Within 20 minutes the police were sitting in my lounge and interviewing Sam.

I gave them Grimson's address and thought surely this time my ex-wife would stop calling her own children "lying little shits".

She'd previously refused to believe that her boyfriend was threatening our children.

The police were involved so maybe this time she would do the right thing.

All Julie had to do was say "sorry boys" and ask for them to forgive her.

She refused.

If my ex-wife had apologised maybe their feud wouldn't still be going on today.

Even after Grimson admitted his guilt to the police she still stayed silent.

Instead of saying "sorry" she continued calling them "lying little shits".

I wondered where was where was her unconditional mother's love, or maternal instinct to protect her children?

The following day we were visited by the police who said:

"We've seen Lucy and can assure you she has not been physically harmed".

Of course I was relieved but asked:

"How could a grown man say such things about a 5-year-old little girl?".

The female officer agreed and said:

"Mr Grimson admitted to saying those things but claimed his was drunk".

Adding:

"We have cautioned and warned him about his future behaviour".

I asked for the response of my ex-wife and what I heard disgusted me.

I was told: "Mrs Johnson didn't believe Mr Grimson would say such things".

I replied:

"But he admitted it."

Female cop:

"I know and we informed her of that but she still refused to join you in pressing charges"

I had to put my liberty at risk. I now had no option but to take the law into my own hands.

There were plenty offers of help from friends seeking revenge on my behalf.

I knew people who knew people.

The chaps, the `proper people` who do not look kindly on any form of child abuse.

One of my oldest friends told his mate, a heavyweight London gangster about my situation.

The underworld legend was both `disgusted and angry`.

I received a phone call inviting me to visit his house and my sons came with me.

We spent a couple of hours in his massive mansion playing pool and discussing my problem.

I gave him a name, a description and an address.

At the end of the meeting he patted both my boys on the head and said:

"Don`t you worry, I`m a dad as well and I`m going to sort it out".

The next night I got a phone call saying;

"We`re outside his house".

Ten minutes later I got another call saying:

"He squealed like a pig"

Adding:

"Tell your boys they won`t be hearing from him again".

And they didn't.

Why is it that bullies are always cowards?

Julie thought he was a tough guy who conned her into believing he was a debt collector.

In reality he was an odd job man and glorified caretaker for a car loan company.

He did have a criminal connection but was no gangster. He was what proper villains call a ponce.

One of my oldest friend`s, a former Detective in the Flying Squad had Grimson`s car registration checked by the police computer.

It revealed that her boyfriend worked as a driver for an Escort Agency in and around Romford who drove prostitutes to meet clients.

Julie Johnson had walked out on her sons to set-up home with a two-bob pimp.

I don't know exactly what happened that night but do know that shortly afterwards he left Wickford.

The rumour is he`s living in Wisbech Cambridgeshire

Julie used every dirty trick in the book and legal loophole to stop me seeing my daughter.

She also stopped Sam and Adam from seeing their sister and my mum from seeing her grand-daughter.

My mum was told:

"You can only see Lucy if my mum and dad sit in on any meeting".

This outrageous offer was rightly declined by my mum who never got on with Julie`s mother.

My mother-in-law from hell and her husband were racist bigots who never accepted me because I was half-Irish.

I had always been the `thick Paddy` who was never good enough for their little girl.

My mum was Irish, I was half-Irish so my 3 children were quarter Irish.

As both boys got older whenever they saw my fascist former father-in-law coming up the drive they`d run upstairs to put on their Irish football shirts.

It was done to wind him up and also as a show of solidarity with me.

They did not like the anti-Irish jokes he made and would often say "were Irish, so he`s also poking fun at us as well".

My mother-in-law from hell, a dead ringer for TV`s Mrs Brown thought she was calling all the shots and enjoying the power she had over my mother.

Or thought she had, as my mum refused to dance to Julie`s tune.

So, like me my mum was denied access to Lucy.

The court cases continued and my ex-wife dreamt up more and more false allegations.

First, I was `mentally ill`, then a pornographic movie-maker and a `bad dad`.

What next?

Unbeknown to me I had mystical powers who behaved like the leader of a cult.

I was portrayed as a Charles Manson type figure.

According to my ex-wife I had brainwashed both my sons against her.

As always Social Services were more than happy to jump aboard her latest bandwagon.

If she`d told Social Worker Peter Brown I worshipped the devil and practised black magic he would have believed her.

No evidence would ever be required and she knew this which is why the allegations became more extreme.

And at the same time more damaging.

When the Hearings for Julie`s allegations switched from Southend Magistrates to the Family Courts in Chelmsford she was handed a licence to lie.

She could now say whatever she wanted because these Hearings were always held in secret and behind closed doors.

I bet Julie now wished she had waited to bring up the subject of her pornographic films.

But at the time she was out of control firing smears in all directions.

Her next list of false allegations once again concentrated on my mental health.

She claimed that in 2002 I was suffering with depression and visited a psychiatrist.

This was a classic case of bending the truth to compromise my credibility.

In 2002 I did seek medical help but for stress not depression and was treated by my GP.

He arranged for me to see a counsellor.

The Family Courts were so corrupt and secretive that not only did they ban the press they banned free speech.

You were ordered not to talk about the proceedings in public or with friends and family.

I was brought up to believe in a free press and an open society so obviously I spoke out.

I informed journalistic friends what was going on.

Mrs Johnson found out and informed the court.

The Judge said I was in contempt of court and sentenced me to 28 days in prison.

Luckily for me and the boys, who on the morning of the case were both in tears, the Judge had a heart and suspended the sentence for 3 months.

I walked from court as a free man.

Julie was not happy. When the Judge said "Guilty" she had a great big smile on her face and looked like she`d won the Lottery.

She almost punched the air in delight.

When the Judge added "suspended for three months" the blood drained from her face and she slumped forward with her head in her hands.

Questions For My Daughter

3rd October 2018

Dear Lucy,

I hope you have read this book with an open mind and in the spirit it was intended.

The aim was to show you that I am nothing like the person you were brought up to hate.

In a way it is both a `love letter` and my CV.

All I ever wanted was for you to know the real me. If you don't like the real me I`ll be heartbroken but at least it will be your genuine opinion.

I`m hoping the truth the whole truth and nothing but the truth will wipe-out the 14 years of brainwashing.

Today is your 18th birthday and hopefully you will want to know your biological Father.

Believe me, it was never my intention to hurt you in any way and I`m talking past, present and future.

Love always

Dad

Xxx

Maybe because I`m the author you rightly or wrongly believe the content of this book is biased in my favour.

So here are some independent views. A leading Academic pays tribute to your dad.

Professor Matthew Worley writes:

"It`s 1981 and Britain is burning. The summer has seen riots break out across the country`s inner-cities.

Newspapers offer stories of `Mob Rule` (The Sun) and a `War on Police` (Daily Mail): roving reporters seek explanation in the `permissive whirlwind` of the 1960s (Daily Express) or the perennial problem of urban decay.

Britain is `close to anarchy`, the Daily Mirror insists, as it juxtaposes images of burnt-out cars and broken windows with a message to the government: `Save Our Cities`.

The realities that lay behind this media vision were complex.

If the 1970s have since become synonymous with acute social tension and political instability, then the 1980s should really fare no better.

For all Britain`s being reinvented as a financial centre geared towards the interests of the entrepreneur (and the flags that flew for the Falklands War), Margaret Thatcher`s premiership was book-ended by recession and disfigured by fierce industrial struggles and social disorder that culminated in the poll tax riots of 1990.

Most disastrously, unemployment became endemic, pushing towards three million in 1981 and rising thereafter.

As always, the young working class were particularly vulnerable to the effects of socio-economic change.

Government policies designed to eschew commitment to full employment in favour of controlling the money supply and `freeing` the market from state intervention and trade unionism ensured many were caught in a toxic combination of deindustrialisation, economic depression and political brinkmanship.

Put together, youthful frustration, social disadvantage and racial tension coalesced to ferment the unrest that scarred the landscape of the Conservatives` promised `new beginning`.

There were many cultural voices that chartered the events of this time.

Punk, reggae and 2-tone, each in their different but often overlapping ways, provided means of social commentary.

Famously, The Specials` `Ghost Town` was number one as the 1981 riots raged.

But others, too, from The Jam through to Linton Kwesi Johnson and Killing Joke, captured the moods and the anxieties that simmered in the proverbial concrete jungle.

Among the most astute was GARRY JOHNSON, whose poems provided first-hand accounts from London`s `dead-end streets`.

Over a series of punk albums released between 1980 and 1984, and in collections such ad Boys of the Empire (1982), he recorded the world as he saw it.

London was a city of tower blocks: `Alcatraz without the rocks`.

The urban back streets became sites of rage, frustration, but also cultural aspiration – where `dead-end yobs` looked to football, boxing or rock `n` roll as a way out from the dole.

He told the truth about power.

The false patriotism of self-serving elites was exposed in a Tory Party that stood `for mass unemployment and poverty, a 'them and us' society`.

Simultaneously, Labour`s transformation from a party built out of working-class communities to a gravy train of professional politicians was spotted early on (1982) via his `Labour MPs Ain`t Working Class`.

Best of all were the character portraits. `The Buzz Kids` and `Young Offenders` getting caught up in the system; the Young Conservatives`, all Daily Mail and bottle-fed: the `boy about town`, head turned by fascist lies, venting his personal insecurities through pointless racism: the `suburban rebel` playing at lefty politics when in college before following their parents into the establishment.

GARRY JOHNSON embodied the punk spirit. Instinctively suspicious of authority in any form, he was nevertheless committed to the DIY ethos.

He was an integral part of the punk scene and street-level rock `n`roll.

Against the class prejudice of a mainstream media that too easily conflated working-class youth culture with racism and violence.

GARRY always presented street punk as an expression of urban protest.

`The white working class has got more in common with the black working class than they have with the rich white middle class.

His was a `street level point of view`, working class kids `having a laugh, and having a say`.

As it was, GARRY – more even than many bands he supported or wrote about – personified one of Joe Strummer`s better insights: `the truth is only known by guttersnipes`.

So you see Lucy I have always been a working class rebel and not the Conservative I was accused of being by your Mother and social worker Peter Brown.

Here is more proof regarding my most popular poem.

An audio track by GARRY JOHNSON, the heavily Cockneyed 'Young Conservatives' which opened the night, could easily have been written the day after the General Election.

June 2015.

The Morning Star Poetry Festival at The British Library.

Roxanne Escoboles

Here is my best-loved poem.

YOUNG CONSERVATIVES
Silver spoon and bottle fed
The Daily Mail is always read
By Young Conservatives born to win
Another world you're living in
Just like your parents and theirs before
You and you children won't go to war
The front line ain't the place for you
You still believe your blood is blue

The British Empire sons and daughters
Who flirt with UKIP's rich supporters
Share nightmares about Tony Blair the Corbynistas on News at Ten
Who want a world where men are men
Money talks and women listen
And missionary is their favourite position

You're born to rule or so you say
Church of England all the way
The book that features Adam and Eve
These are the things that you believe
Young Conservatives dressed to thrill
In army clothes they shoot to kill

Love and respect for king and queen

National Service at Seventeen
Mary Whitehouse morals too
A Barbara Cartland novel view
These are the things that you support
The working class they must be taught
How lucky they are to be free
To live in our democracy
With no free press or radio
Thousands homeless and millions on the dole

Just like the days before the war
The Tory Party still stands for
Mass unemployment and poverty
A `them and us` society
With no tower block kids to tell the truth
Only the voice of Tory youth

The House of Lords, the den of vice
Vermin in ermine ain`t very nice
The wealth the power the lady on the throne
All the land they stole and own
The red the white the Tory blue
The Young Conservatives I hate you

So, you see Lucy I really wasn't a conservative voter like your mother`s right-wing Father which is why we always clashed.

Apart from your mum we had nothing in common.

I was much more than a former teenage tearaway.

I was also a genuine working class rebel who all his life supported the underdog and flirted with the world of showbiz.

Don't just take my word for it, here is my first-ever interview from Sounds music magazine.

`The geezer in the shabby jacket with the speed freak frame and impish smile knocks back his lager and pulls a bundle of tatty A4 exercise books out of a plastic bag at his feet.

They`re choc-a-bloc with poems, all painstakingly written out in longhand.

"I've got about 300 of `em," he laughs, "I reckon about 50 are good."

Honest, self-effacing GARRY JOHNSON. It`s hard to believe this skinny herbart who lists his likes as `lager, football, rebels, gangster movies and the opposite sex`, as a potential voice of a generation.

Yet those who`d criticise New Punk as having nothing to say could do little better than check out his verses, proud prole manifestos that pull no punches, tolerate no hypocrisy and tell no lies.

And that`s not just my opinion. Listen to Time Out`s review of Garry`s `Boys of the Empire` collection:

"A pamphlet of ballads, streetwise, anti-militarism and fascism, anti-police and fiercely defensive of working class pride.

Very impressive."

Natch, they omitted to mention his dislike of trendy lefties too.

"I didn't even think they`d read it, a bloody posh paper like that," Gal laughs.

"What do they know about kids on the street?"

Born in Hackney, Johnson grew up in London`s East End, getting a comprehensive non-education (six schools, one expulsion) and clocking up DC and Borstal with convictions ranging from robbery to burglary via such naughtiness as taking part in a riot and bunking fares, though he`s not been nicked since he was 17.

Despite a promising start as a schoolboy footballer, he began working life as a builder`s labourer.

"I was originally inspired to start writing by Janet Street-Porter," Gal reveals laughing, "That, and then the New Breed bit in Sounds last year"

Despite his hatred for the Tories, police harassment et al, Johnson remains equally dismissive of the Labour Party, as illustrated by poems like `Labour MPs Ain`t Working Class`.

"I think in some ways Labour are worse than the Tories," Gal opines, "Cos you expect Tories to be the enemy, they always have been, always will be, but I hate Labour more because they`ve let us down the most.

They`re supposed to be for working class people but in power they`re just as anti-working class as the Tories."

`Boys of the Empire` is his only `product` at the moment, though he`s working on a collection of prose and poetry with Cock Sparrer`s Garrie Lammin, and a skinhead collection provisionally titled `How To Live In A Police State`.

He made his record debut on Strength Thru Oi (to high praise from punk visionary Valac Van Der Veena) and bega live performance with a short well-received recital at The Deuragon in Bethnal Green.

Now The Business could be putting a couple of his hard-hitting poems to music too.

There's little doubt in my mind that GARRY JOHNSON will develop from the Linton Kwesi Johnson of punk into a much wider recognised figure, spraying words like machine gun bullets to tear through class injustice and establishment cant.`

So you see Lucy I have never changed. I still stand by every word of that article from 30 years ago.

Back then I was trying to get into showbiz and still am.

POETRY IN MOTION was the headline for my second Sounds interview with Johnny Waller.

He was not impressed with my shambolic lifestyle and liberal use of drugs.

`The way of life for celebrated Punk Poet GARRY JOHNSON seems to be one of glorious chaos, rarely sleeping in the same place twice in a row and taking as much speed as possible.

"Got any Wrigley's, John?" he enquires as I question him on the beginnings of new Street Punk. Were all the bands friends before the `movement` came into being?

"Nah, not really. Like The Business are from the other side of the water – the posh side (he means south of the Thames) - Johnson himself hails from the East End.

"None of the groups knew each other at all".

GARRY became involved through his song lyrics which he'd been writing ever since he was in a group called Joey Teen and The Buzz Kids, "I was the only one who wanted to take it seriously," he complains, "At school, English was the only thing I was any good at besides football.

Now when I write, I do two versions – one as a poem, the other as a song with a chorus."

It's one of those song versions `Suburban Rebels` - which is currently part of The Business's set and under consideration as a future single.

JOHNSON meanwhile has his own plans to go into the studio with a backing band to record a couple of songs for single release.

So how does he see things developing?

"Most of my poems/songs are about keeping hold of what you`ve got, holding on to what you already have gained, `cos if Thatcher had her way, we`d lose it all and they`d bring back National Service.

The lyrics are representative for those who take Street Punk seriously, those who were into Punk.

Perhaps there`ll be a new Sex Pistols or Clash coming through soon...perhaps The Buzz Kids might be it".

The Buzz Kids, it should be explained, is Johnson`s own fledgling group!

Describing himself as "an ex-skinhead, waiting for something else now".

He occasionally seems disenchanted with Street Punk already, reckoning that `Glam Rock` might return.

"I hope so. If it was like Mott The Hoople, it would be great – Ian Hunter`s lyrics are brilliant."

His favourite album of all-time is still `The Rise And Fall Of Ziggy Stardust And The Spiders From Mars` and his infatuation soon becomes even more obvious "Just call me the `Bowie of Street Punk` he says, "I used to write a hundred different versions of `Ziggy Stardust` but I`m holding them all back until the revival."

Are you a talented instrumentalist like Bowie?

"No - he`s a genius. I`d just like to be. I can mime to all his records though."

It`s doubly ironic that this IMMENSELY LIKEABLE unemployed `Jack the Lad` has both the talent and respect of others to become the focal point of the Street Punk Movement, but fritters away his time and energy on drugs and daydreams.

Having long ago given up hopes of a job - "I used to try really hard, but I got turned down by Fords, British Rail, the Post Office...so I thought `sod it`."

He`s virtually retreated to his world of words and abdicated his right to any position of prominence he might have attained.

His marvellous book of lyrics `Boys of the Empire` is full of biting sarcasm aimed at social injustices, and if they occasionally seem clichéd and riddled with a quaint class consciousness, that can be overlooked since – for him – IT`S ALL TRUE.

But, for all his rabble rousing and brave intentions, it amounts to nothing more than empty words if JOHNSON doesn't back it up with action.

He should be actively encouraging new bands, speaking as a passionate yet rational leader of a movement that desperately needs to focus on positive attributes before it crumbles under the weight of its ow doubts and contradictions, with its detractors waiting to bury it – alive if need be.

GARRY JOHNSON with the comparative freedom of being an individual (one might almost say a CELEBRITY even) rather than a member of a group – should be prepared to make a stand, to clearly clarify media misconceptions, to organise Street Punk benefits, to speak out against violence and fascism.

He should be attempting to right some of the wrongs which he so bitterly despises.

Instead of merely complaining.

Do you vote, GARRY?

"No, never. I suppose I'm a working class Liberal – I really like old TV programmes like 'When the Boat Comes In' - when the working class united.

I don't like party politics or the Royal Family. If I was in charge of this country I would break up the United Kingdom, give England it's own parliament and legalise fast drugs".

It's a crying shame because Punk Poet GARRY JOHNSON could have been a contender.

He could have been a spokesman for a generation...but prefers having a laugh to storming the barricades."

So, you see Lucy I wasted my talent as I preferred partying to building a career.

But confirms I still believe in exactly the same things I believed back then.

From David Bowie to a Working class revolution.

Lucy, my third interview with writer Jerry Harris was published in Punk Lives magazine and is proof that 'drugs don't work'

Billy Wizz had been replaced by Charlie and as you can see, my ego was out of control.

Jerry wrote:

"GARRY JOHNSON, the self-styled `Cockney Dylan`, is about to explode back onto the punk scene with the release of his debut EP `The Empire Strikes Back`, which finds the working class hero backed by some of the biggest names in New Punk.

JOHNSON`S no stranger to Street Punk aficionados.

He wrote the best-selling `Story of Oi` paperback and his poems appeared on both Strength Thru Oi and Carry on Oi albums.

For many people he seemed to disappear during 1984 and early 85, but in reality JOHNSON had been hard at work.

He performed on stage as a poet and fronted his own band The Buzz Kids, at one-off gigs around the provinces, also finding time to write his first play, `The Clash`, with the help of BAFTA award-winning playwright Tony Marchant.

He also auditioned for a part in Marchant`s play, `Thick As Thieves` but says, "I turned it down because I didn`t want to get a crop."

He left crops and spikes behind years ago, "Punk is a state of mind," he says, "not how you look."

In recent months Johnson has been back writing witty reviews for Sounds, He`s been screen-tested for a role in a US film along updated `Bronco Bullfrog` lines after an American producer caught his `James Dean` like (he grins) performance in the Canadian TV documentary `A Day In The Life Of A Beat Street Poet`.

He`s also written a new volume of punk poetry, a follow-up to his critically-acclaimed `Boys of The Empire`, which`ll come out the same time as his EP record.

A versatile character or what?

To understand what makes him tick, let`s start at the beginning.

The only son of a Cockney song and dance man, Johnson`s road to Rock & Roll was a roller-coaster ride, making it via Football, teenage delinquency (a string of DC`s and Borstal) and teenage boredom.

"I went from Georgie Best to David Bowie," he grins, "Once I heard Ziggy Stardust, I hung up my football boots and bought a guitar."

The tattoo on his right arm says it all: `Sex & Drugs & Rock`n`Roll`.

The interview took place in the heartland of Johnson`s territory, barely half a mile from the West Ham United Football Ground.

You`ve got two tracks on the `Son of Oi` album?

"Yeah, that's right, good ain't they?"

I've heard the album and they rank amongst the best stuff.

"Thanks Jerry, I'd been told you was a man of taste."

What do you think of the album as a whole?

"I like it, Street Punk has found its feet again. Paranoid Pictures and Prole are the best new bands."

You actually appeared on stage with Paranoid Pictures.

"Yeah that's right, I Thurrock. They're very talented, a bit too much like Siouxsie And The Banshees, but they'll go far.

Though on the night I blew 'em off stage."

What about the other poets on the album like Attila the Stockbroker?

"What about him?

No seriously, if I was deaf and dumb I'd buy all his records."

What other punk poets do you rate?

"Dunno about punk, I rate Linton Kwesi Johnson, John Cooper Clarke, Tim Wells and early Dylan."

But they're all the old guard, what about the new wave like Seething Wells and Joolz?

"Wells no way, he's so dogmatic it hurts, Attila's serious stuff is okay, but his so-called funny poems have got all the humour of a burning orphanage.

The only one to watch is Billy Bragg from Barking – he's a real working class punk."

How did you come to write for Sounds?

"They needed me!

Robbie Millar liked my style and she liked the cut of my trousers.

No seriously, my friend and mentor Garry Bushell encouraged me to write."

Bushell has featured heavily in your career?

"Yeah, well, there is a lot of him, but he has played a very major role, yeah.

He pushed me all the way and really helped when I've gone off the rails.

I'd like to say 'thanks' in print of that's alright, 'cos he's a great bloke."

As your mentor, what deals has he got you?

"Well as you know, the two tracks on the Son of Oi album, plus the latest book and EP."

Is it a rant record of just you?

"Oh no, it's a real rock & roll record, real street anthems."

Who's backing you, The Buzz Kids?

"On one track, yeah, but I want variety, every track will be different.

One punk, one Ska, a poppy track and a poetic rap.

Tom of The 4-Skins is playing bass, Steve Kent from The Business on guitar, a couple of chaps from Cock Sparrer with guest vocals from Lee Wilson of Infa Riot.

It's a toss-up whether Frankie Flame or Mick Ronson (Bowie's old sidekick) produce it."

What happened to John Muir and Babylon Books who published `Boys of the Empire` and `The Story of Oi`?

"I am still working with them. I've got a David Bowie and Glam Rock book coming out early next year.

But I'm keeping my poetry, music and songwriting separate."

Any future plans?

"What, apart from the film?"

Yes.

"Well I want The Buzz Kids to be a permanent gigging band because it's really important that the message of my lyrics is heard by a wider audience.

Even more so now that The Jam have split and Weller has abdicated.

There's a vacuum to be filled and, in my modest opinion, the record buying public need me as much as I need them."

You sound a bit big-headed, Gal.

"Yeah, but I you've got it flaunt it."

So finally, who do you rate at the moment?

"The Alarm are superb, The Redskins because `Lean On Me` is a classic, so good it could have been written by me.

I also like U2, Hanoi Rocks and of course David Bowie is still the main man.

As writers go, no one has come close to the Holy Punk Trinity of Julie Burchill, Garry Bushell and Tony Parsons.

If you had writers that good at your magazine you'd be laughing."

LUCY.

A few months after that interview, my life changed. I stopped believing my own publicity and writing punk poems, reverted to being a Mod and blagged my way into Fleet Street.

White lines didn't kill me but they did kill my creative energies.

I became lazy and more interested in partying than writing anthems or making music.

It was the end of the Punk Poet and the beginning of a decade as a showbiz writer and tabloid hack.

Life After Death

Like our saviour Jesus Christ, I rose from the dead, only I went one better and did it twice.

After 29 days in a coma and on a life support machine I spent two months in rehab learning to walk, talk and think again.

My memory was a mess and couldn't even remember the lyrics of my favourite songs like `Ziggy Stardust` and `Anarchy In The UK`.

I'd also forgotten that my dad was dead even when he visited me as a ghost.

As I was regaining consciousness I thought could feel his hand on my shoulder and smell his aftershave.

I could hear him urging me to get better saying `come on Gal you can do it`.

When I told my sons about his `visit` I was shocked to be told he'd been dead for three years.

The long road to recovery was not easy and it would be months before I was able to think clearly.

A doctor suggested I start writing lists. Then I started to write poetry and short stories to exercise my brain.

One of those short stories became my debut novel Serial Killer and is now being made into a Hollywood movie.

If that sounds far-fetched I suggest you Google Sandie West Beachdancer Films Serial Killer.

Sandie is the producer of the film. As I stated earlier I always seem to connect with the opposite sex

My publisher Teddie Dahlin is also female.

At the time I was given legal permission to tell my story I wasn't well enough to continue fighting my ex-wife for contact with my daughter.

I was warned the stress would kill me.

I decided to concentrate on getting fit and healthy but like a old retire boxer I wanted to have one last fight.

The fire was burning in my belly.

As Judge Moloney had previously warned Essex Social Services:

"Mr Johnson is like a dog with a bone and will not go away."

I tried again for contact but this time Peter Brown was nowhere to be seen.

Essex Social Services had been replaced by a more private and sinister organisation.

My ex-wife had teamed up with Caffcass.

If Social Services were the Gestapo this mob were a combination of ISIS and the Taliban.

They were a Government sponsored organisation more secretive then The Freemasons.

I was visited by 2 of their charmless stormtroopers before I got to court and told:

"Mr Johnson you seem vulnerable and not fit enough to see your daughter"

They were blaming me for looking like a warmed up corpse and undergoing two triple Heart bypass operations.

It was my fault I`d `died` twice and been in a month-long coma.

But these people are selected because they have no hearts, compassion or humanity.

As with the Nazi war criminals at Nuremberg their mantra is "we were only following orders".

But whose?

When they arrived at my front door they had documents from Essex Social Services and instructions from my ex-wife.

They were either neutral or impartial.

Social Worker Peter Brown had falsely accused me of being `mentally ill` and now CACASS were attacking me for looking like death warned-up.

The meeting lasted no more than 15 minutes.

A week later I got a letter saying "we will not support you seeing your daughter."

I expected that but not the content of the second paragraph.

It claimed:

"We have visited Lucy who told us she does not want to see you."

I was in a state of shock and momentarily in a deep depression.

It broke my heart.

This was the first time I'd been denied contact directly by Lucy and not via my ex-wife.

I phoned my sons saying: "I'm going to fight this" but they talked me out it.

To be honest I didn't have any fight left in me. I already had a dodgy heart, damaged liver and broken kidney.

My duty was to stay alive for Sam and Adam. I could not risk my health by taking on my ex-wife, Cafcass and the courts.

What would be the point if my daughter genuinely didn't want to see me?

I hardly spoke, ate or slept for a week.

Why did she hate me?

Was the brainwashing that bad?

I decided to write this book so Lucy Johnson would know her real dad and not the character described by my ex-wife and former in-laws.

I wanted to make her proud so re-wrote Serial Killer almost line by line before sending it to my publisher.

I'd faced death five times and lived to tell the tale. Instead of using all my energy going to court.

I would write a book.

A message to my daughter.

The problem was it would be four and a half years before she became a woman.

I had a grown-up story to tell that could only be told to another adult.

What could I do to keep my brain ticking over and my heart beating?

As luck would have it and with perfect timing I was contacted by Swedish rock star Soren Sulo Karlsson.

Fate stepped in, as it started to do on a regular basis and within weeks I was in a recording studio with former Clash drummer Terry Chimes, top record producer Kevin Poree, Idde Schultz and Sulo.

The Swedish rocker gave my punk poems a rock & roll makeover and we recorded the album `Punk Rock Stories And Tabloid Tales`.

Music mogul John Dryland was so blown away Cargo Records gave us a three-year deal.

The album was critically acclaimed with a five-star rating in Sounds.

I was well happy. I thought my daughter has got to be impressed with this.

It was all over the Internet and I appeared in various newspapers and magazines.

I put messages to get in touch on Facebook and Twitter but she didn't make contact.

This was followed by a book `Punk Rock Stories And Tabloid Tales` highlighting my past as Punk Poet and performer.

I was featured on TV, the radio, my local paper, magazines and The Daily Mirror.

But no word from my daughter or was there?

I got a few cryptic messages on Facebook, an email and a Tweet but no actual contact.

When Serial Killer was finished I sent it to my publisher Teddie Dahlin who loved it.

A copy found its way to Sandie West at Beach Dancer Films in Little Venice, Hollywood and the rest as they say is history.

My story featured all over the media but still no word from my daughter.

So, I decided to contact her by writing this book.

What did I have to lose?

I'd rather she disliked the real me then hated the made-up character invented by my ex-wife and former in-laws.

Apart from not knowing each other personally we have no idea what the other sounds like.

What are my thoughts?

I hope we share the same personality but not the accent.

I wonder if you are rebel, anti-establishment and a free spirit like your dad.

I would love you to be a non-smoker.

A veggie and an animal lover.

I do hope you don't like football but love the Arts.

Are you a music lover?

Do we share any interests?

What is your favourite film, TV show or book?

Here are a few facts about your dad.

Hero David Bowie.

TV: The Office, The Inbetweeners.

Film: The Man Who Fell To Earth.

I`ll tell you the rest when we meet.

So Who is Your Dad

So, who is the author of this book?

Garry Johnson is one of Punk Rock's most enduring and colourful characters.

He first appeared as a Poet in the 1980s and has since been a singer, rock & roll manager, a showbiz journalist and songwriter.

More recently he has found a new level of fame and admiration as a co-songwriter with Swedish rocker Soren Sulo Karlsson and for surviving 5 heart attacks and 2 life-saving triple heart bypass operations.

His has been a life lived on the edge.

A real-life x-rated soap opera lived in the glare of publicity.

He travelled from the back streets of East London, to West End clubs and The Houses Of Parliament.

Garry is a genuine Cockney Rebel who infiltrated Fleet Street and the world of showbiz.

He met everyone from David Bowie to Michael Jackson.

A man described by music writer Dominic Warwick as "Charles Dickens for the Punk Generation".

Gal's words painted vivid pictures of rebel youth growing up in a world populated by low-life politicians.

His poems and song lyrics were a window to a teenage underworld of unemployment, violence and fast drugs.

But he balanced that nihilism with a passion for life and a raging social conscience.

Garry hated bigotry as much as he despised what passed for authority.

He was the real voice of the street and his book of poems 'Boys Of The Empire' is considered a classic piece of writing.

Garry Johnson was/is a fanatical seeker of truth and justice.

A passionate believer in the truth, the whole truth and nothing but the truth.

He used that life-long passion to take on and defeat Essex Social Services.

Garry went `face to face` with social worker Peter Brown and as you know by reading this book he won.

If anyone wants to contact me for interviews or to read any of the documents mentioned in this book my email is:

GarryJohnson230@outlook.com

Me and Mr Brown

Social Worker Peter Brown criticised me for as he put it "focusing" on the abuse suffered by my 3 children.

Did this insensitive bastard attend the same training college as the Social Workers who covered-up for the North of England grooming gangs?

This man had no interest in the truth and refused to consider the feelings of my children.

I asked:

"How would you feel if your children were violently threatened and verbally sexually abused?"

He always refused to answer the question.

Dealing with Mr Brown as it was with all social workers was very frustrating.

Unlike the police they refused to allow any of our interviews to be recorded.

They relied on notes which were always a figment of their imagination.

From day one I hated Brown and believe me the feeling was mutual.

At first because of my thick Cockney accent he treated me like a working class criminal.

It didn't help that I looked like Ray Winstone and walked like Danny Dyer.

My ex-wife told him I was "mad, bad and dangerous" and instantly he hung on her every word.

I'm convinced Julie looking like Patsy Kensit at her peak played a massive part in conning Mr Brown.

At first as with the police he was like `putty in her hands`.

She charmed the pants off him using all the acting skills learned in movies like `Saturday Night Specials`.

It took 5 years before the Social Worker would see through her lies and beg me for help.

We were no longer Mr Johnson and Mr Brown as former enemies were now on first name terms.

He turned up on my doorstep requesting a favour.

"Garry will you please help to get Mrs Johnson off my back?"

Adding:

"She's still making allegations".

I remember laughing as seeing him so stressed really amused me.

He wanted me to see a high-profile Forensic Psychiatrist who specialised in seeing serial killers and convicted psychopaths.

Adding:

"I know there's nothing wrong with you, but it will really help me out.

If you can convince a Forensic Psychiatrist that your not dangerous it will shut Mrs Johnson up.

It will get her off my back".

I was not keen as I'd already been giving a `clean bill of health` by two psychiatrists.

The Essex Criminal Mental Health Team and 2 doctors at Bellmarsh maximum security prison.

I'd already suffered 5 years of mental torture, persecution and fighting-off false allegations.

Brown assured me this would be the final hoop to jump through.

I'd heard it all before and said "No".

He begged me to sleep on it.

I decided to seek advice.

I contacted 3 people involved in my `long fight for justice`.

My legal adviser.

An old friend and former Flying Squad Detective.

My local MP.

All advised me to do it for the same reasons.

I had nothing to hide and nothing to lose.

But was that true?

What if Essex Social Services rigged the result or refused me a copy of the report.

I would only agree if I got certain conditions put in writing.

1. The Forensic Psychiatrist selected would be independent of Essex Social Services.
2. I would get a copy of the report.
3. The verdict would be final

I got written assurance so agreed to be interviewed.

The examination was intense and detailed.

It lasted 2 hours and after a stress-full Eight week wait a copy of the report was hand-delivered by Mr Brown.

It confirmed what I already knew.

I was not mad, bad, dangerous or mentally ill.

I asked:

"Is that the end of the matter?".

He wouldn't be drawn but it certainly changed the dynamics of the relationship.

Sam never saw him again.

Adam only a few times.

I only saw him when attending court for contact with my daughter.

My local MP was very happy with the result and revealed the report would have cost Essex Social Services in the region of £7,000.

Fatal Attraction

Why if we had such an idyllic and perfect marriage did it end in a bitter divorce?

Well, maybe in a way it was my fault.

True it wasn't me who had a fling with part-time football trainer and full-time copper Ian Fleming.

Or an affair with self-confessed child-abuser Richard Grimson.

But such is my character and addiction to honesty it`s only fair that I share the blame.

I wouldn't say Julie was a sex addict but she was highly sexed.

Some people are hooked on drugs, alcohol, gambling or all three.

Luckily for me she was addicted to sex.

To quote the Buzzcocks song she was an "orgasm addict".

And for 14 wonderful years I was more than happy to feed her addiction.

It suited me perfectly as I got the benefit of her insatiable appetite for sex.

But at the end of the day her constant cravings destroyed our marriage.

She was an addict who needed her fix and I wasn't supplying her drug of choice, so maybe that is why she chose another supplier.

As this book is not meant as a `whitewash` of me or a `character assassination` of her I am duty bound to tell the truth, the whole truth and nothing but the truth.

Regardless of it embarrassing her or humiliating me.

When we both had high sex drives everything was fine but mine faded.

A year before she left there were early signs of future heart trouble.

I had no idea this would lead to 5 heart attacks and two triple heart bypass operations.

This added to my stress levels lowered my sex drive.

I lost interest in everything from making love to making porn films.

It drove her into the arms of others.

I never told her about my chest pains or money problems. So, in a way I am to blame for her infidelity.

Julie sought affection from other people because wrongly she thought my lack of interest in her meant I must be seeing another woman.

That was so untrue as I was 100 per cent faithful throughout the 15 years we were together.

I was on medication and the first time the tablets `kicked in` I couldn't `rise to the occasion`.

Julie was naked and `gagging` for it and let's just say she was not happy.

If talking about her porn movies made her blush, now it's my turn.

Let's just say that when I got on top I couldn't perform.

For the first time there was no life in my wand, her pet name for my manhood.

The more I tried the floppier it got and the more she moaned, not in pleasure but in anger and frustration.

I was sweating as if I'd just got out of the shower.

She called me every name under the sun, and how can I say, finished the job herself.

Sadly, the same sort of thing happened a few more times and I honestly believe those embarrassing incidents convinced her to be unfaithful.

It wasn't another women that came between us it was the early stages of a medical condition that would end with me spending 29 days in a coma.

Throughout our 15 years together Julie was up for everything and I never complained.

What bloke would?

She loved dressing up and playing games in the bedroom so life with her was never boring.

The truth is I never stopped loving my wife or got tired of having sex with her.

She was all I ever wanted which is why I never cheated, or even thought of cheating.

Julie had a favourite saying and position.

It was: "I want to take you to the Derby" which was her on top and impersonating a jockey.

She enjoyed taking control and being in charge and I never complained.

As to be honest I had nothing to complain about.

My ex-wife had a thing about her bum and to be perfectly honest so did I.

It was apart from her long blonde hair, perfect figure, longs legs, heart-of-gold and sense of humour her most prized possession.

Without sounding soppy or like a wimp it took me years to get over her leaving.

It wasn't just the sex. I missed her friendship as much as I missed her body.

I thought of her every day and dreamt of her every night.

I missed the laughter, conversation, watching TV and bringing up our 3 children together.

She wasn't just my wife, lover, mother of my children. She was also my best friend.

The perfect soulmate.

I missed mundane things like sharing a bar of chocolate or packet of crisps.

Watching her get dressed, yes, I did say "getting dressed" as Julie got dressed in a very special way.

She was just as sexy putting on her underwear as taking it off.

I missed looking at her in the bath and the way she toweled herself dry.

Blow-drying her hair and putting on her make-up. The truth is I missed everything about her.

The best way I can describe how I felt when she left, it was like losing a 'loved one' to cancer.

It was as if she was dead and that day a massive part of me also died.

I would mourn the loss of my wife, marriage and family life for many years to follow.

I could write thousands of words about my perfect wife but that isn't what this book is about.

I could write a Mills and Boon style love story and predict a happy ending.

I could say I never stopped loving her. It would please and amuse her, but such is the change in her personality I fear she would laugh and consider it a sign of weakness.

The Julie Johnson of today is not the person that I knew and loved for 15 years.

That person has gone forever and will never return.

Witness of Abuse

Why was I the only one concerned about the safety of my children? Social Services claimed I was obsessed but then Sam, Adam and Lucy were not their children.

My hatred of child abuse and child abusers was nothing new. It went back years.

I didn't just hate evil perverts like Ian Huntey, Myra Hyndley and PAYNE.

I had personal reasons to hate rapists and paedophiles.

Once by accident I witnessed a sexual attack. I was also a victim.

Aged 12 I witnessed a gang of older boys stripping a 15-year-old girl naked.

A year later I was sexually molested in a Children's home.

I went to quite a few schools, so there's no danger by recalling this incident that I'll reveal the identity of the victim.

It was a sunny Sunday evening and I was taking a short cut home through the local park and came across a gang of 15 and 16-year-old boys from my school.

There were 8 or 9 of them and recognised some as older brothers of my mates.

As I got closer I could see what was going on, they were keeping watch while 4 others attacked a defenceless girl.

They had her pinned to the ground and were removing her clothes.

I was shocked at seeing these bullies groping and grabbing her.

I wasn't sure of her name but did recognise her face from school.

What I witnessed stayed with me as did the feeling of guilt for not stepping in to help.

Years later I saw the same girl at a friend's birthday party and felt very awkward.

I was terrified in case she recognised me as the skinny little kid who saw her naked.

Today as an adult, if I came across such an incident I'd automatically step in.

It was witnessing that attack which inspired my novel Serial Killer.

A story of revenge where a teenage rape victim waits 20 years to wipe-out a gang of rapists.

I was also a victim during my first stay as Boyles Court Children's Home in Brentwood Essex.

My abuser was not a gang of teenage boys. He was a Ronnie Corbett lookalike with an Elvis Presley quiff.

By coincidence, it also happened on a Sunday night.

This could explain why I've never been a fan of Sunday evenings.

It has nothing to do with TV's Songs of Praise, but I'm sure it's due to flashbacks of those incidents.

I still remember both incidents as if they happened yesterday.

The bastard came into the dormitory, sat on my bed and put his hand on top of the duvet just inches away from my private parts.

I can still see his face and smell the aroma of Brylcreem in his hair.

I returned to Boyles Court a year later, this time more like a young man than a little boy.

This time I was a big cocky skinhead and immediately sort him out.

Let's just say he kept his distance and didn't come back for a second grope.

I despise both child and sexual abuse.

That's why I got so angry when the perverted boyfriend of my ex-wife violently threatened and verbally sexually abused my three young children.

I told all this to Social Worker Peter Brown but still he and The Family Courts couldn't, or rather wouldn't understand my genuine hatred of abusers.

Lightning Source UK Ltd.
Milton Keynes UK
UKHW041622231118
332780UK00001B/49/P